D0744605

NOV   2007

How the Quakers
Invented America

Books by David Yount

Author:

GROWING IN FAITH
A Guide for the Reluctant Christian

BREAKING THROUGH GOD'S SILENCE
A Guide to Effective Prayer

SPIRITUAL SIMPLICITY
Simplify Your Life and Refresh Your Spirit

TEN THOUGHTS TO TAKE INTO ETERNITY
Living Wisely in Light of the Afterlife

BE STRONG AND COURAGEOUS
Letters to My Children about Being Christian

WHAT ARE WE TO DO?
Living the Sermon on the Mount

FAITH UNDER FIRE
Religion's Role in the American Dream

THE FUTURE OF CHRISTIAN FAITH IN AMERICA

CELEBRATING THE REST OF YOUR LIFE
A Baby Boomer's Guide to Spirituality

Translator:

J.-C. Barreau & D. Barbe,
THE PRIEST TODAY
His Mission and Witness

Pierre Talec,
CHRISTIAN PRESENCE IN THE NEIGHBORHOOD

How the Quakers Invented America

David Yount

ROWMAN & LITTLEFIELD PUBLISHERS, INC.
Lanham • Boulder • New York • Toronto • Plymouth, UK

Some of these essays originally appeared in slightly different form in Friends Journal, Quaker Life, Potomac Review, The Washington Post, and in my syndicated column for Scripps Howard, "Amazing Grace."

ROWMAN & LITTLEFIELD PUBLISHERS, INC.

Published in the United States of America
by Rowman & Littlefield Publishers, Inc.
A wholly owned subsidiary of The Rowman & Littlefield Publishing Group, Inc.
4501 Forbes Boulevard, Suite 200, Lanham, Maryland 20706
www.rowmanlittlefield.com

Estover Road
Plymouth PL6 7PY
United Kingdom

British Library Cataloguing in Publication Information Available

Library of Congress Cataloging-in-Publication Data:
Yount, David.
 How the Quakers invented America / David Yount.
    p. cm.
 Includes bibliographical references and index.
 ISBN-13: 978-0-7425-5833-5 (cloth : alk. paper)
 ISBN-10: 0-7425-5833-9 (cloth : alk. paper)
 1. Society of Friends—United States—Influence. 2. Society of Friends—United States—History. 3. United States—Church history. I. Title.
 BX7635.Y68 2007
 289.6'73—dc22

                                                                    2007006135

∞™   The paper used in this publication meets the minimum requirements of American National Standard for Information Sciences—Permanence of Paper for Printed Library Materials, ANSI/NISO Z39.48-1992.

In memory of the first Quakers,
who called themselves Friends of the Truth
and sang joyfully in their prison cells

"Life in America was to give new meaning
to the very idea of liberation. . . . The Quakers
possessed a set of attitudes which fit later textbook
definitions of American democracy."
—Daniel J. Boorstin

Contents

A Tale of Two Quakers

*W*hen the bullet-torn body of American Quaker Tom Fox was discovered in a rubbish-strewn Baghdad street in March 2006, the news made front-page headlines around the world. The American's hands were still bound, and he bore evidence of torture inflicted by the Iraqi dissidents who had abducted him.

Three fellow peacemakers—a Briton and two Canadians—had been kidnapped by the same terrorists but were later released by them. Fox alone was murdered precisely because he was an American.

The news media were quick to identify the middle-aged husband and father as a Quaker pacifist. But he was far from an ideologue. Whereas hard-core pacifists distance themselves from violence, Fox sought it out as a peacemaker. He had been a member of the Christian Peacemaker Team, an American-sponsored group of 150 volunteers seeking reconciliation in the world's trouble spots.

Fox's captors, who called themselves the Swords of Righteousness Brigade, justified the kidnapping to press for the release of all prisoners in Iraq, but they were also open to taking ransoms for their prisoners. They separated Fox from his fellow hostages, who never saw him again.

Tom Fox was a convert to the Quaker faith, having joined the Northern Virginia meeting to which my wife and I belong. In the company of other Peacemakers, he roamed Iraq unguarded in an attempt to assist Iraqis of hostile sects to reconcile with one another. As a diplomatic mission, Fox's effort clearly failed, but it was only an attempt to apply American ideals of comity to another people.

Rather than dismiss Fox as a starry-eyed pacifist who merited his fate for placing himself in harm's way, he is better appreciated as the latest in a long line of Quakers whose ideals of fairness, equality, and community launched the creation of the United States and formed the American character. Tom Fox did not proselytize a religious faith; he was simply a true American.

So, too, in his way, was Nathaniel Greene some 230 years ago, although Greene's idea of peacemaking was to create concord by defeating the oppressor by a call to arms. A Rhode Island Quaker, Greene had never seen battle when, at the age of thirty-three, he became George Washington's most trusted general. At the time he was commissioned, all Greene knew about warfare he had learned from books. Yet he created the most disciplined troops in the Continental army and was instrumental in the British retreat from Boston, the American defense of New York, and success at Princeton and Trenton.

Greene was the first of the generals to call for American independence before its declaration by Congress. He wrote to Philadelphia early in 1776, "Permit me then to recommend from the sincerity of my heart, ready at all times to bleed in my country's cause, a Declaration of Independence, and call upon the world and the great God who governs it to witness the necessity, propriety and rectitude thereof."

Greene's civilian aide was Thomas Paine, the author of *Common Sense*, the most widely read pamphlet published in colonial America. Paine, himself raised as a Quaker, was the most articulate advocate of American independence.

Greene, the Quaker, justified fighting as self-defense: "We are soldiers who devote ourselves to arms not for the invasion of other countries but for the defense of our own, not for the gratification of our own private interests, but for the public security." Until the British escalated the war, Greene, like his commander in chief, sought peace and harmony between the mother country and the colonies. Alone among Washington's generals, Greene served for the full term of the war.

At the time of Valley Forge, Washington confided that, should he be killed or captured by the British, Greene, the Quaker, should take his place at the head of the army. When Washington survived, Greene was given command of the Southern army, driving the superior forces of Cornwallis to Charleston, where they remained until war's end. His success in the South set the stage for the last major battle of the Revolution at Yorktown, Virginia, and subsequent victory and independence.

Tom Fox, the pacifist Quaker, and Nathaniel Greene, the fighting Quaker, both exemplify an America whose founding ideals and national character stem from the Quakers. In the following pages, I trace that legacy and introduce you to the people who converted America to their ideals.

Preface

There is a sense of timelessness about the Friends Meeting House off old Route One in Alexandria, Virginia. The simple frame dwelling with its wide verandas has stood on the same property for over a century and a half. Faded photographs show the building to be unchanged since the Civil War, when soldiers paused on the porch to carve the names of wives and sweethearts on the door frames and Union pickets occupied the building.

Within the meetinghouse, the only evidence of time passing is an old regulator clock that ticks with every transit of its pendulum. It is the only sound in the great open room where local Quakers worship in total silence, many with eyes closed against a world they believe moves too quickly and inconclusively. For an hour each First Day (Sunday) morning, some hundred Friends seek there a sense of permanence in the stillness.

Here gathered are lawyers and journalists, lobbyists, and federal staffers and their families, briefly abandoning the rat race of life in the nation's capital in favor of savoring an eternal moment. Few of them find meditation to be easy, but they persist week after week.

There would be nothing pernicious about time if people possessed the knack of living fully in the present instead of dwelling on the past and fretting about the future. My dogs and cats instinctively possess that ability. People have to learn it.

It's well worth the effort. You and I can at least *attempt* to control the present, whereas our pasts are lost and our futures uncertain. Happily, there is no room for regret or anxiety in the present moment.

Poets celebrate its immediacy, seeking to freeze its riches in their verse. "Stay," they plead against the passing of time. "Stay, you are so lovely!"

History can be defined as time unraveling itself. As one pundit put it, "History is one damn thing after another." Even today's newspaper is irrelevant, valuable only for recycling, because it chronicles what has already happened and cannot be undone.

But Quakers cherish the present, which is the only permanence of which anyone can be certain. That may explain why all contemplative people are content: they cherish the present moment and mine its treasures, whereas the discontented welcome the passing of time, hoping something better will come along later. Their hope, alas, is only seldom rewarded.

Time, the critic Herbert Spenser noted, is something most people try to kill, concluding wryly that time ends in killing them. Time is the certain messenger of mortality, ensuring that one day we will all be singing "The September Song." When pubs close in England, the proprietor urges his customers, "Hurry up, it's time!"—an announcement that could make a fitting epitaph for frenetic lives. "Time goes, you say? Ah no," Robert Browning lamented. "Alas, Time stays, *we* go."

Happily, there is an alternative to time and its ravages. It is eternity. The vast majority of humankind, through all ages and cultures, have treasured the expectation of an afterlife. More than nine of ten Americans now living express the faith that they will join all those who have ever passed through life, to reach a state where time no longer reigns. Shakespeare himself insisted that time must have a stop. It ends in eternity, which—far from being an endless extension of time—is a perfect *now*.

Contemplatives are not the only humans who seek a taste of eternity in their present lives. The intensity of the present moment can be realized on a roller coaster or in the throes of sexual ecstasy, in free fall, or in Bach's "Goldberg Variations." Thrill seekers and aesthetes alike are masters of life in the present tense; so are naturalists and even gardeners— so absorbed in the present moment that time effectively stops for them.

Once, as a foolish young man, I came close to drowning in a lake in upstate New York. In my desperation, contrary to legend, I did not review my past life. Instead, I was totally absorbed in my predicament. It was a scary kind of timelessness.

Religion popularly views eternity as *escape* from time and change, from regret and anxiety. But it is more than a respite; it is fulfillment.

"Teach us to care, and not to care," T. S. Eliot prayed; "teach us to sit still"—because in stillness we see clearly. The Sabbath is a reminder of eternity, contrived to be a day of rest, reflection, and retreat.

Lamentably, even those who worship with others of their faith on the Sabbath often discover that the experience affords paltry opportunity for reflection. Churchgoers are too busy praying aloud, singing hymns, listening to sermons, and catching up with their friends to quietly catch up with themselves and eternity. For that, they need time alone and a place apart, as the Quakers have, escaping time (at least briefly) through silence. "Be still," urged the psalmist, "and know that I am God."

Before clocks became common, people noted the passing of time only by light and darkness and the cycle of the seasons. During the Ages of Faith, few knew the month or even the year. There were no alarms, but only the *Angelus*, sounded when the sun was directly overhead. Before electric light, in a world lit only by fire, a winter's night could be fourteen hours long—too long for sleep—and the absence of artificial light left few options. Accordingly, quite ordinary people rose in the middle of the night to pray, savoring the stillness and sensing eternity.

Those transcendental meditators who lack a foundation in religious faith find a timelessness in their reveries, but religion insists that eternity is *real*—indeed, that it is more real than time. Time is partial, while eternity is complete. The monastic life was designed specifically for men and women who abandoned time for eternity. To this day, monks are unwilling to wait for death for the curtain to be raised on eternal life, opting instead to live in its light now.

When I was researching my book *Spiritual Simplicity*, I paid a visit to the Trappist monks in Berryville, Virginia, to experience how they manage simultaneously to keep one foot within time and the other in eternity. Incidentally, they claim no copyright on that ability but welcome visitors of all faiths (and none) who seek a respite from time, however brief, for a taste of eternity.

Holy Cross Abbey is home for life to twenty men, whose ages I reckon to range between the late twenties and early seventies. Fourteen white wooden crosses in the monastery's yard are mute reminders that some of the monks have already passed definitively from time to eternity.

Forget your mental picture of dour medieval monasteries derived from Hollywood epics. Holy Cross looks more like a summer camp and consists of simple sprawling white-frame buildings. The chapel where monks chant the Divine Office daily at intervals between 2 A.M. and 7 P.M. resembles an airy dining/recreation hall at a kids' camp in the Catskills.

But there are no noisy campers here. It is a place of utter silence, serenity, and decorum. At sunrise, the monks' soft chant competes only with the lowing of cattle in the fields. Until the 1960s, Trappists spoke to one another only in emergencies, otherwise relying on simple sign language. No longer so constrained, they still find little to say to one another but much to say to God.

I was able to entice the retired abbot, Father Mark Delery, into talking to me one autumn morning. Before he became a monk, Father Mark was a physician, and he still keeps up with the medical journals. The old abbot had just returned from his own annual retreat, which he spent alone in a cottage on the New Jersey shore. "Even a monk needs a change of scene and a break from routine to clean out the cobwebs of habit and regain perspective," he explained.

The only indication that there is a monastery in the rolling, green, uncultivated Virginia countryside is an inconspicuous placard nearly three miles from the highway. Yet the guest book in the abbey's retreat house testifies that men and women from New York and beyond have discovered it and stayed. Many leave testimonials to their few days' respite from the rat race.

"Home again," one retreatant wrote of her experience. Many unsolicited testimonials repeat the same words: "peaceful," "restful," "blessings," and "gifts." One pronounced his retreat "rejuvenating," another "cosmic." Most guests exult in their escape from time and say so. Breathing the fresh air and absorbing the serenity of the Shenandoah Valley, they rediscover the miracle of life and proclaim it to be wonderful.

Stepping aside from duty and the expectations of others to take a fresh look at their own lives, they begin to shed the dead ballast of prejudice, scrape off the barnacles of pointless habit, dismiss empty illusions and hopes, abandon false pride, regain courage, and get back to the practical pursuit of a simpler life. Like a time machine, the abbey transports its visitors, but not to another time. Rather, it freezes time in a moment that mimics eternity.

Welcoming retreatants is neither a mission nor a business of the Trappists. Holy Cross monks subsist by operating a bakery on the grounds that sells bread through area supermarkets and holiday fruitcakes by mail order. But monasteries have always welcomed the pilgrim from a world obsessed with time—an open secret that spreads by word of mouth to this day. Originally, the monastery's visitors were housed in a primitive farmhouse, but the demand became so great that in 1985 the monks built a modern brick-and-concrete retreat house with sixteen spartan but comfortable single rooms, a library, a dining hall, a kitchen, and a chapel. Each retreat house room has a window with an unobstructed view of the Shenandoah foothills. Buster and Rosemary, two large gray farm cats, are silent presences. They keep the house rodent free.

"Half our retreatants are repeaters," Father Mark admits, "but we make room for newcomers by not allowing regulars a second visit within six months." The monks do not inquire about their guests' religious beliefs, but Father Mark reckons that fewer than half are Catholics, and all are seekers in some sense. He told me the story of a visiting Quaker who sensed the presence of restless Civil War dead on the property. The visiting Friend spent his retreat praying to pacify the spirits and encouraged the monks to join him, promising that the abbey would be more peaceful and attract more members.

"And do you know, he was right!" the old abbot exclaimed with a twinkle in his eye.

Father Mark, now retreat master, resists taking preformed groups. Groups of people who require the company of others to escape time can meet anywhere, he believes. "They don't need this place," he says. "What you need to accomplish here you do best on your own." Some visitors come in hopes of confronting chronic problems, but the monks do not encourage guests with acute or severe crises. "We're simply not equipped to help them," Father Mark confirms. If they choose, retreatants can confide in him and receive his guidance, but they are not obliged to follow it. Although he is a physician, he writes no prescriptions and provides no nostrums, pharmaceutical, psychological, or spiritual. A monk's retreat lasts a lifetime, so the former abbot feels no rush to suggest shortcuts to eternity.

Nor is Father Mark a guru. Each retreatant must confront his own demons and angels to work out personal solutions. Most visitors, he relates, arrive with clear goals but without strict agendas for spending their vacation from time's demands. Many come with a book they have always wanted to read, or they find one in the library. Most hike up to the monastery chapel several times a day to hear the monks sing to God. There isn't much else to do in this quiet, isolated place except take long walks through the fields and along the river. No radios, no television, no magazines or newspapers—nothing to remind one of the passage of time except the rising and setting of the sun.

The poet Robert Browning insisted against time's devastation that "the best is yet to be." If that is your expectation (as it is mine), then our present journey is only a prelude to be lived in the prospect of eternity. For millions of credible persons now living, the afterlife is not just a hopeful hypothesis but an actual experience. Somehow revived after having been medically dead, millions of men, women, and children report not only that death is kind but that eternal bliss awaits. They know, they insist, because they have been there. Having resumed their earthly lives within time, they are transformed, living not for the present but in the light of eternity.

Astronomer Carl Sagan was an expert on living. In fact, he contributed the article "Life" to the *Encyclopaedia Britannica*. Yet several years before Sagan's death in 1996, he suffered a near-death experience—and spoke well of it. "I would recommend almost-dying to everybody," he said. "You get a much clearer perspective on what's important and what isn't."

Sagan agreed with the counsel of the medieval *Ars Moriendi* or *Art of Dying*: "Learn to die and thou shalt learn to live." It is a lesson well learned by those who have briefly tasted eternity without a touch of morbidity. They gain an appetite for living, give generously of themselves, and anticipate their definitive demise with an equanimity, hope, and confidence that the rest of us can only dream of acquiring. Because they have been to the edge already and found the journey exhilarating, they do not fear the return trip.

While recent authors who have made their near-death experiences public are often inarticulate in attempting to explain their extraordinary visions outside time, others before them described their *real-death* experiences poignantly. With his last words, Thomas Edison reported that "it is very beautiful over there." "I've never felt better," confided Douglas Fairbanks. "I feel myself again," said Sir Walter Scott. Elizabeth Barrett Browning's final word as she met eternity was, "Beautiful!" Goethe exclaimed, "More light!" Chopin observed in his last moment of time, "Now I am at the source of all blessedness." Rousseau, ever verbose as he ran out of time, urged those who attended him to "See the sun, whose smiling face calls me; see that immeasurable light. There is God! Yes, God himself, who is opening his arms and inviting me to taste at last that eternal and unchanging joy that I have so long desired." These celebrated men and women, who had made the most of their time this side of eternity, nevertheless took leave of this life with the conviction that they were entering a better one.

Short of leaving time and being transported to eternity in a near-death experience, Quakers anticipate it through immersion in the present moment. So can you.

This is not as mystical as it may appear. We cannot prepare for eternity unless we cultivate the habit of living, loving, and exhausting the present. That is what it means to be alive each moment.

Christians regard resurrection as fact rather than wishful thinking. Resurrection is humankind's common aspiration. As the phoenix rose from the ashes of its own destruction, so we humans expect our spirits to rise in a new creation, unburdened by time, regret, and anxiety. In such an eternal state, intimacy will no longer be rare and reckless, but the standard for all relationships. Pain and age will pass. As time ends, disappointment will disappear. We will survive life's struggle, and love will last.

When Albert Einstein was asked what lay beyond infinity, he replied simply, "The face of God." St. Paul conceded that, confined as we are by time, we view reality as in a distorting mirror, but he promised that in eternity we will see clearly. Despite our present lack of complete clarity, it makes sense to plan our inevitable journey now by living in eternity's light.

Quakers are so fixed on silence and simplicity that you may know nothing of them. They do not proselytize, and, compared with other denominations, they are not numerous. So the smiling man on the oatmeal box may be the closest look you've been afforded of these "peculiar people." Still, they are neither shy nor elitist. And they are quietly significant, having been honored with the Nobel Peace Prize and having played a critical role in the creation of the American nation and character.

You don't have to become a Quaker to borrow some practical wisdom from them. Consider this your invitation.

Introduction

"Convincement"

In place of the word "faith," Quakers prefer to speak of their "convincement." It's a quaint word you won't find in an ordinary dictionary, but it means that Friends are convinced of their beliefs to the point of confidence. Their religious faith is neither simply an inheritance from their family nor a mindless habit. Rather, they have had to expend some effort in the search for religious faith and become persuaded of what they believe.

No one expressed the meaning of "convincement" better than St. Paul in his letter to the Romans:

"For I am convinced that neither death nor life, neither angels nor principalities, neither present nor the future, nor powers, neither height nor depth, nor any other creature, will be able to separate us from the love of God that comes to us in Christ Jesus our Lord" (Romans 8:38–39).

Few people, I suspect, aspire to become persuaded in quite the way Paul was: struck by lightning, thrown from his horse, and temporarily blinded. But many aspire to Paul's "convincement."

I am a latter-day Quaker but a birthright Christian, baptized in the earliest weeks of my life, when my parents and godparents proclaimed a faith for me that I could neither express nor understand as an infant. Still, even as a child I became a believing Christian long before I became a convinced Quaker.

Convincement consists, I believe, in about equal parts of intellect and emotion. Authentic Quaker spirituality maintains that balance. As a Friend, I do not affirm my faith aloud in the words of the Nicene Creed every week as many other Christians do. But I do believe much more than just what I feel, and I trust what I believe: that God is not simply an inner presence but the creator of all that is, whose Son was sent to live and die for us, to save us from ourselves, and to reveal what God-likeness is. The better I grasp who God is in himself, the better I am able find God within myself and to serve him in others.

I cherish all that I learned about God in the years before I became a Quaker, and I carry it all with me, unalloyed and undiminished. A member of our meeting has characterized most of us as "renegades" from other churches and denominations. In that sense, although I am a convinced Quaker, I am not a convert. To *convert* means literally to turn around one's life, and I haven't strayed from my past convictions. I have been on this path all my life. But I have found my home among Friends at path's end.

It is a home marked by simplicity, not austerity. Quakerism is easier to define by what it is not than by what it is. Friends have no church, no clergy, no sacraments, no sermons, no liturgy, no art or statuary. In their place we treasure the silence, and we have each other. We have hymns but prefer stillness. We honor the creed but do not make its words a test of our loyalty. The Scripture plays a substantial part in my life, but I don't carry a Bible around with me as a talisman. When Quakers gather together to pray in silence, none of us knows the words the others are using.

So long as Friends don't identify "the God within" as their personal possession, they are on safe ground. Religion is full of temptations to eccentricity. When Moses left the Israelites in the desert, he discovered on his return that they were worshipping a golden calf. Ever since, Jews and Christians alike have had to fight the temptation to attach their faith to something more palpable than their invisible God. That is known as idolatry, and it is forbidden by the Second Commandment.

The genius of Quakerism is that its simplicity removes many things that people might be inclined to substitute for God: sacraments, the liturgy, the creed, hymns, sermons, sacred art, proselytism, and the Bible itself. As the early Quaker theologian Robert Barclay noted at the time of the Reformation, many Christians of the time were clinging more to words of Scripture than to the Word of God, which is Jesus. As Friends of the Truth, Quakers are spared those distractions.

To be sure, that does not make them superior to other persons of faith but less inclined to fool themselves that they are being faithful when they are merely being pious and sentimental.

Many Friends describe their spiritual life journeys as "searching." I'm inclined to believe that it is instead a simple acceptance of being "found." In poet Francis Thompson's vision, all peoples are pursued throughout their lives by the hound of heaven but attempt to elude our common Creator by distraction, indifference, and self-love. "Be still," the psalmist counsels instead. "Be still and know that I am God." For it is in the stillness that God speaks to us.

Of course, simplicity makes sense only when there is something to simplify. Children aren't drawn to simplicity but rather to piling up treasures of knowledge and experience (not to mention adventure and mischief). Eventually, each of us "comes of age" when we have absorbed enough to develop distinct personalities and abilities. Then, as adults, we start to sort out our treasures, deciding which are most desirable, discarding or setting aside other goods from our attic of experience, and establishing priorities. As one wise feminist cautioned her ambitious sisters, "Yes, you can have it all, ladies, but not all at the same time."

My eldest daughter, now an adult, has been plagued since childhood by attention-deficit disorder—a condition marked by difficulty in sorting things out and attending to one thing while disregarding others. For victims of this syndrome, everything demands equal attention. Those who are hard of hearing and require hearing aids encounter a similar problem. When I pay attention to just one voice, I automatically shut out competing noises—the tick of a nearby clock and the sound of traffic outside. Unfortunately, hearing aids give all sounds equal weight.

Some Quakers are inclined to define simplicity as making do with less. In any case, it does not require us to live spartan lives. One can live simply yet comfortably. Once, when I was interviewed about a book I had written on the subject, I was asked to name a celebrity who leads a simple life. I answered, "Donald Trump." Why? Because that multimillionaire lives *simply* for business: to make deals. Most of us are not only poorer but more scattered in our attention.

Successful people determine what really engages them, then discard competing interests. You may remember when Michael Jordan attempted to be both a successful basketball and baseball player. He was only mediocre in the batter's box and soon returned full time to what he did best. No one thought any the less of him for simplifying his life.

The U.S. Declaration of Independence affirms that each of us enjoys a God-given right to pursue happiness. It does not pretend to tell us what happiness consists of, so we all choose our own prescriptions over a lifetime. I believe that only God, who owns the patent and holds the blueprint to all creatures, knows what will make us happy. He alone, as our creator, knows what makes us tick. St. Augustine concluded that human hearts will be restless until they rest in God.

When I was researching my book *Spiritual Simplicity*, I came across a study by a social scientist whose specialty is happiness. What he confirmed was that happiness is not a consumer good—not a pot of gold at the end of the rainbow. Rather, happiness consists of its pursuit, the process of purposeful living. Simplicity helps us be happy because it cuts the clutter from our hearts and minds and allows us to concentrate on what really matters.

Silence is a radical kind of simplifying. In silence you and I are aware of all the competitors for our attention, learning with difficulty to discard the nonessentials. I am drawn to the Quaker practice of sharing the silence with one another. Each of us individually is a solitary animal, unable to communicate our pain and pleasure to others. But we can demonstrate our solidarity as children of the same God in the same silence. That makes us Friends.

I am an only child. At home I grew up in the company of my parents, so "family" was never a big thing in my experience. But friendship was—and is—and I do not take friends for granted. Quakerism attracts me not least because it allows me to regard myself as a Friend and to count on other Friends.

Originally, Quakers were known as Friends of the Truth, but they have always been Friends to God, to one another, and to every living thing. I have sensed that bond wherever I have traveled within and outside the United States. For Friends there are no strangers.

The poet Coleridge referred to friendship as "a sheltering tree." That's how I like to think of it. I am grateful to make my extended family among Quakers, who help me along my journey. I feel blessed to be able to call them Friends.

How the Quakers Invented America

> Be examples in every country, place, or nation
> that you visit, so that your bearing and life
> might communicate with all people.
> Then you will happily walk across the earth
> to evoke that of God in everyone.
>
> —George Fox

$\mathscr{A}$t some point in their schooling, American children are taught that our nation's founding principles were borrowed from the European Enlightenment. No effort is made to explain how purely secular roots could give rise to the spirituality that has always pervaded American life.

Any unprejudiced reading of American history reveals that America was founded by peoples who sought freedom to practice their particular religious faiths. The vaunted American tradition of church–state separation exists to guarantee freedom of religion, not its discouragement, and to mandate religious tolerance by all peoples.

Moreover, the overwhelming religiosity of the American people continues to serve as a bulwark protecting democracy, the rule of law, trial by one's peers, consent of the governed, universal education, and equal opportunity. Far from being the products of secular minds, these innovations were successfully incorporated into colonial life by a religiously motivated people as early as a century before the American Revolution.

Quakers, the most harshly persecuted Christians in seventeenth-century England, found refuge in Pennsylvania, founded by William Penn, himself a member of the Society of Friends. Over time, Pennsylvania became the model for the United States. The liberty that Americans take for granted originated not in the minds of secular Enlightenment thinkers but from the application of the Quakers' Christian faith.

It is no coincidence that the American Declaration of Independence was proclaimed in Quaker Pennsylvania or that our young nation's Bill of Rights was modeled after the Quaker-drafted constitution of Rhode Island. The Liberty Bell itself, which rang to celebrate the Declaration of Independence, was originally the Great Quaker Bell, purchased by the Pennsylvania assembly long before the American Revolution.

"Proclaim Liberty throughout all the land unto all the inhabitants thereof" was inscribed on the bell by Quakers before freedom was proclaimed to be the right of all Americans. As early as 1682, William Penn, in the preface to his *Frame of Government for Pennsylvania*, had announced that "any government is free to the people under it (whatever be the frame) where the laws rule, and the people are a party to those laws, and more than this is tyranny, oligarchy, or confusion."

Former Librarian of Congress Daniel J. Boorstin affirms that "the Quakers possessed a set of attitudes which fit later textbook definitions of American democracy." Despite their relative obscurity in twenty-first-century America, Quakers, by dint of their role in forming the American character, can be said to have invented America.

To this day, all Americans subscribe to the following fundamental beliefs of the people who call themselves "Friends."

EQUALITY

Boorstin quotes a 1757 sermon in Maryland by the Quaker "saint" John Woolman: "Though we made Slaves of the Negroes, and the Turks made Slaves of the Christians, I believed that Liberty was the natural Right of all men equally." The Friends' sense of equality was radical for its time, extending to women, African Americans, Native Americans, and, in the early Quaker expression, "the Turk and the Jew."

INFORMALITY

To this day, people around the world still marvel at the typical American's candor, lack of ceremony, and straightforwardness. The Quaker sense of simplicity in dress, manner, and language was quickly adopted by their fellow countrymen and women and continues to this day.

TOLERANCE

Because Quakers held that there is "that of God in everyone," they made no doctrinal demands on others, welcoming cultural and religious differences as God-given rights of conscience.

Less obvious than these foundations of the American character, Quakers strongly influenced how Americans speak, regard sex, marriage, and child rearing, name things, build their homes, dress themselves, and eat and work and how we approach death and define social status and power. Some examples follow.

PLAIN SPEAKING

The majority of Quaker immigrants came from England's North Midlands. They brought their way of speaking with them. Historian David Hackett Fischer characterizes it as "a muscular speech—bluff, literal, direct, vivid, forceful, and plain-spoke. It has strong and simple ways of saying things, and little use for the learned niceties of Latin and French."

Unlike regional American dialects that still persist in New England and the Deep South in the twenty-first century, the English spoken by colonial Quakers employed expressions, pronounced vowels, and stressed the same syllables we find in standard American speech today.

"Let your words be few," Friends decreed against the flowery extended rhetoric of aristocratic immigrants to the colonies. The notable exception, the use of the familiar "thee" and "thou" by Quakers in the early years, was intended not to be quaint but as a social equalizer—no person more exalted than another. Even the welcoming of Native American words and place-names into the American vocabulary can be traced to the early Quakers. William Penn himself learned to speak the language of the Algonquins in order to converse with them in their own tongue. More Indian place-names were retained in Quaker Pennsylvania than in the other original colonies.

HOME CONSTRUCTION

Early in the colonial period, Quakers set the pattern for American home building, using durable materials and seeking spaciousness and comfort consistent with simplicity. In this, they were not inventive but merely mimicked home construction in England's North Midlands—favoring stone walls, slate roofs, and wood trim. By contrast, homes in early New England were rambling wooden structures. Even in aristocratic Anglican Virginia, which favored decorations, home-building materials were less permanent.

Visitors to George Washington's Mount Vernon are invariably surprised to note on close inspection that the mansion's apparent brick exterior is in fact only wood siding coated with sand to give the structure a more permanent look. In Virginia's fine colonial homes, interior doors were cut from ordinary pine but carefully painted to resemble the graining of more expensive woods. The Quakers preferred simple, solid construction to superficial decoration.

FAMILY LIFE

According to historian Barry Levy, Quaker communities were "the first scene of a major, widespread, obviously successful assertion of the child-centered, fond-fostering, nuclear family" that characterizes American family life today. Contrary to the prevailing colonial spirit, love was the spiritual cement of the Quaker family, and the household was regarded as a union of individuals equal in the sight of God.

Whereas Puritans and Anglicans alike employed fear to maintain family unity, Quakers repudiated it altogether. They valued the family as a spiritual communion whose primary role was raising its children and promoting the spiritual health of all its members.

THE IDEA OF MARRIAGE

Quakers believed that marriage should be founded in true Christian love, which is giving. Unlike many early Americans, Quakers held that love must precede marriage, not follow it. It should be a union of "sweethearts," a term they often used. They forbade dynastic marriages of first cousins, which were then common in Virginia, and even discouraged wedlock between second cousins. Believing that marriage is integral to the health of the broader community, they required the entire community to be witnesses to the marriage bond. When William Penn wed Gulielma Springett in 1672, there were forty-six witnesses to vouch for the union. In turn, the newlywed couple's home was often built for them by Quaker neighbors.

EQUALITY OF THE SEXES

The early Quakers held that "in souls there is no sex." Accordingly, women became ministers, preaching equally with the men. They were also persecuted equally. My wife has written about colonial Quaker women who were imprisoned, beaten, abandoned to the beasts of the forest, and even executed for having the temerity to speak up for their faith. The Quaker Mary Dyer, having defied a sentence of banishment from Massachusetts, was hanged on the Boston Common to become America's first martyr for religious freedom.

Quaker men and women worshipped together, separating only to transact the meeting's business. This was not segregation but merely an accommodation for women to discuss their own concerns. Quaker men considered their wives to be equal rulers and heads of families with them. "They are helps-meet, man and woman," Quaker founder George Fox declared.

The feminist movement in the late twentieth century promoted gender-inclusive language, something that was already routine in the colonial period among Quakers, who employed the double pronoun "he and she" instead of the generic "he."

AMERICANS' NAMES

Like many twenty-first-century American parents, Quakers tended to name their firstborn children after grandparents, honoring paternal and maternal lines equally. The eldest son was typically named for the mother's father, the eldest daughter for the father's mother.

Unlike the Puritans, the Quakers did not favor biblical names. John, Thomas, William, Joseph, and George were favored names for boys; Jane, Catherine, Margaret, Mary, Anne, and Elizabeth were popular for girls in Quaker families. All remain common names for Americans born in twenty-first-century America.

CHILD REARING

Quakers were unusual in claiming that children were born innocent. Many of them rejected any notion of original sin, a doctrine that their philosopher Robert Barclay dismissed as "unscriptural barbarism." Most Friends believed that children were incapable of sin until they were old enough to understand the consequences of their behavior. Youngsters were not only a delight to their natural parents but prized by the entire community, which sought to shelter them from the world and create a secure environment in which they could mature.

Even when children reached the age of reason and were tempted to act rebellious, Quaker parents resisted corporal punishment. As William Penn urged, "Love them with wisdom, correct them with affection: never strike in passion, and suit the correction to their age as well as fault. Convince them of their error before you chastise them . . . punish them more by their understandings than the rod."

Accordingly, Quakers preferred parental rewards to punishments and promises to threats. In this they were supported by the entire community of Friends acting as an extended family. Quaker children were taught obedience to conscience rather than to persons, and parents were scrupulous about not choosing favorites among their children, treating them instead as equals in respect and affection. At a time when youngsters were often sent away to pursue apprenticeships, Quaker parents did all they could to keep their children at home or at least nearby.

RESPECT FOR CHILDREN

Mary Dyer, facing execution by hanging at the hands of the Boston Puritans, was asked if she wished a Quaker elder to pray for her. "Nay," she

said, "first a child, then a young man, then a strong man before an elder."
It was an eloquent reflection of Friends' belief in Jesus' proclamation that
unless we become as little children, we cannot enter the kingdom of
heaven. Quaker elders fashioned themselves not as patriarchs but as
"nursing mothers and fathers," keen to teach the child to follow God's
leading. Because Quaker children were not kept subordinated to elders,
some of them—boys and girls alike—entered the Quaker ministry even
before they reached adolescence, reminiscent of the boy Jesus convers-
ing with the teachers in the temple in Jerusalem.

OPTIMISM

In colonial times the average American seldom lived beyond his or her
mid-thirties. Death was as familiar as life, often the consequence of accident and disease rather than old age. A certain fatalism pervaded even observant Christians, but for Quakers it was tempered with optimism. Death
was not to be feared but welcomed as the curtain-raiser on eternity.

Accordingly, Quakers discouraged wakes and long periods of
mourning, opting for simple funerals and preferring memorial services.
The current fashion among Americans mimics the colonial Friends, with
funerals a private affair and celebratory memorial services welcoming
family, friends, and associates of the deceased. When Susan B. Anthony
planned her own Quaker funeral, she insisted, "Let in the light," forbid-
ding mourning dress and insisting that there be lots of bright, pretty
flowers.

CONGREGATIONAL WORSHIP

Quaker meetinghouses were functional structures, unrelated to church
architecture. The buildings managed to be simple without being austere,
intended for meditation, featuring many large windows and white-
washed walls to capture the light and dispel the gloom. Churches of all
denominations in America today tend to mimic Quaker simplicity and
the value placed on natural lighting. Economy of construction is one
driving force, of course, but the other is that the building is meant for
group worship, not just individual inspiration.

SPIRITUALITY VERSUS SUPERSTITION

Satan was downplayed if not utterly dismissed in Quaker faith. "We have not hoofs nor horns in our religion," the early American Friends said. Unlike Puritan Massachusetts, Quaker Pennsylvania dispensed with laws against witchcraft because Friends denied magic (black and white) and superstition. Quakers held that evil was the product of man, not Satan, and often the product of carelessness and ignorance rather than malevolence.

The Friends' upbeat spirituality, however, allowed for healing and miracles through the Spirit and sought after perfection of character during one's lifetime. Such was their reverence for life that they became unusually concerned for the welfare of animals, some of them suspecting that reincarnation was possible between and among the species. The great Quaker painting *The Peaceable Kingdom* reflected the Quaker belief in peace among all creatures as normative in nature.

THE VALUE OF EDUCATION

It is sometimes alleged that the early Quakers were disdainful of formal education, but in fact they were critical only of education that was frivolous or merely speculative because they believed such schooling caused divisions among people rather than bonding them.

William Penn stressed practical education: "Let their learning be liberal. Spare no cost . . . but let it be useful knowledge such as is consistent with truth and godliness, not cherishing a vain conversation or an idle mind; but ingenuity mixed with industry is good for the body and mind too."

In England, which was saddled with an established state religion, Quakers were deemed Nonconformists and prohibited from participating in political life, attending the great universities, and entering the traditional professions. Friends were even required to be buried apart from loyal adherents of the Church of England. As a consequence, they made their mark in science, engineering, medicine, banking, management, and industry, as well as in agriculture, becoming successful entrepreneurs and often surpassing aristocrats in wealth.

In America, Friends were not officially confined to practical professions, but American schools themselves expanded their curricula beyond the humanities into science, technology, and practical professions. So education in America today is much as the early Quakers wished it to be to best serve all students.

SIMPLE LIVING, SIMPLE PLEASURES

The early Quakers even anticipated our contemporary do-it-yourself American culture. Simple, sensible diet and comfortable everyday clothing were the norms. "Enough is as good as a feast," they believed, as they promoted moderation, and they decried anything like keeping up with the Joneses. To be sure, temperance did not equal prohibition but merely moderation. One ate to live rather than lived to eat. Health-conscious, diet-happy contemporary Americans tend to agree.

Quaker "plain dress" was little more than a reaction against class pretension and frivolous fashion in the colonial period. It was not a uniform but simply the choice of comfortable, practical clothing. George Fox pointed to the irony in the Bible that clothing itself was a consequence of shame, prompting man and woman to cover their nakedness, but had led to fashionable clothing becoming decorative. Plain dress, incidentally, was not necessarily of cheap manufacture. Quakers chose the best-quality fabrics they could afford. Benjamin Franklin, ever the politician, is often mistaken for a Quaker when in fact he only aped plain dress to impress Friends in Pennsylvania society.

Today, all Americans prefer casual clothing as comfortable and practical.

SPORT AND LEISURE

In contrast to the colonials, contemporary Americans have expectations of being entertained when at leisure.

Today's couch potatoes would not get high marks from the early Friends, who discouraged idleness, ball games, hunting (except for food), horse racing, and even the display of animals in zoos, faulting captivity as harmful to the beasts.

On the other hand, Quakers mandated physical education in their schools and were among the first Americans to promote swimming and ice skating as healthy sports. They also favored gardening as a "gentle recreation."

William Penn, as usual, had the last word. "The best recreation," he said, "is to do good." In this respect, the Quaker character has rubbed off on *all* Americans, who are noted universally for their philanthropy and volunteerism.

WORK

For Quakers, work was a fundamental form of worship, the service of God through one's God-given talents. Penn remarked that even Quakers in prison managed to devise ways to keep working. For them being occupied was a matter of discipline—of taking control of one's life. Still, the early Friends were far from workaholics, nor did they labor from ambition or a desire for wealth. Even as many Quakers became affluent, they retained their simplicity of life.

The business ethic practiced by every individual Quaker was considered to reflect on all Friends. Accordingly, local meetings assigned committees to ensure honesty and fairness, not unlike Better Business Bureaus today or the Good Housekeeping Seal of Approval. Their insistence on fair competition, pricing, and truth in advertising presaged the development of chambers of commerce across America.

Bankruptcy was considered a moral failing among Friends, reflecting irresponsible spending and investment. Still, Quakers were quick to help those who had fallen on hard times without requiring them to go to creditors who took advantage of their predicaments. To this day, cooperative credit unions manage to lend money cheaply, and the government treats bankruptcy humanely.

Because they made a practice of helping one another, Quakers became pioneers in the insurance industry. The oldest corporate business in America—founded in 1752—was a Quaker cooperative that insured against loss by fire. Back in England, Quakers became financiers through their Lloyd's, Barclay, and Gurney banks. Philadelphia remained America's most prominent capital market until surpassed by New York in the nineteenth century.

VALUING TIME

Anglicans spoke of "killing time" and Puritans of "improving time," whereas American Quakers set themselves to "redeeming time"— managing it usefully. But they were not workaholics. "Busyness is not our business," Penn advised.

During their revolution the French awarded time new names, purging the old Christian calendar. By contrast, Quakers purged the Christian calendar of its pagan references, referring to the days of the week and months of the year by number rather than by the sun, moon, planets, and pagan gods. In their place, the Quaker Sunday became "first day" and January "first month"—a custom that persists among them to this day.

Moreover, they abolished many religious and secular holidays, including Christmas, reasoning with Robert Barclay that "all days are alike holy in the sight of God" and worthy to be celebrated. Friends did not idolize time but merely sought to use it well. Not for them was the Puritan notion that "time is money." Rather, Penn said, "Time is what we want most, but what, alas, we use worst, and for which God will certainly most strictly reckon with us when time shall be no more."

WEALTH AND POVERTY

Quakers disdained clannishness. William Penn aimed at creating an all-inclusive society of independent farm families (Quaker and non-Quaker alike) that was neither rich nor poor. In his own Pennsylvania, he was remarkably successful. As early as 1715 there was not an acre of unsettled, unproductive property within fifty miles of Philadelphia. Penn also ensured that Pennsylvania's inheritance laws left no one destitute by decreeing equal shares for all children. Typically, daughters, instead of inheriting active farmland, were given "portions" when they married, also receiving a share of the personal estate.

This insistence on fairness ensured sufficient affluence from generation to generation so that Friends felt comfortable leaving substantial charitable bequests in their wills, and survivors continued their philanthropy during their own lifetimes. Historian David Hackett Fischer believes of the early Quakers that "no other English culture was so strongly committed to philanthropy, and their charity extended to everyone in need, not just to needy Friends."

This Quaker virtue continues to be integral to the American character in the twenty-first century. Today, poorer Americans consistently contribute a larger proportion of their income to charity than their wealthier countrymen and women.

SOCIAL STANDING

Contemporary Americans have long since distanced themselves from the time when the lowly born, poor, uneducated, manual worker was expected to show deference to his "betters." If a remnant of "class" still exists in America, it is stratification by material wealth and nothing more. But we all have inherited the Quakers' insistence on egalitarianism in American society.

Quakers substituted the simple handshake for all the bowing, scraping, curtseying, and hat tipping that was expected in social deference at the time. They refused to call anyone "master," "mister," "sir," or ma'am," let alone "Lord" or "Your Grace." Instead, they greeted everyone, Quaker or not, as "Friend."

SOCIALIZING

The colonial Quakers were determined to be good neighbors, both to fellow Friends and to others, but they were far from social butterflies. They were content with their own company and that of their families, joining others for useful projects that benefited the community. For them, personal honor consisted of integrity, not chivalry, saintliness, or etiquette.

Today, Quakers are probably best known for their peace testimony, a cause dismissed by many Americans as utopian. But not all Quakers are ideological pacifists. Rather, they seek peace by means of conflict resolution. A Friend of mine lobbies persistently for the creation of a federal Department of Peace that would enjoy the same standing as the Department of Defense. Many members of Congress, including a recent candidate for president, have embraced the cause. Conflict resolution, far from being a pipe dream, is more science than art and is already successfully employed in cases coming before state and local courts in the United States. The United States Institute for Peace is a federal agency in Washington that actively promotes peaceful solutions to world conflict.

The Quaker preoccupation with peace stems from George Fox's imprisonment in a dungeon by English Puritans for refusing to fight at the battle of Worcester in 1651. William Penn, renowned as the greatest swordsman in Ireland, also refused any call to violence. Quakers believed that peace was something everyone sought, defined minimally as one's responsibility not to intrude on the quiet of another person. Peace was the state of orderly living, based on conscience, the golden rule, and the presence of God in everyone, including antagonists.

Of course, the unwillingness of Quaker legislators to provide for the defense of their fellow citizens led to their removal from Pennsylvania politics. But on a local level, they were successful is assigning trusted persons to be "justices of the peace" to resolve conflicts. Moreover, Quakers were warned against being litigious and appealing to the civil courts with their disputes. Instead, their meetings tended to reconcile differences among members. However, Quakers were quick to punish in law those who trampled on the private rights of others.

CRIME AND PUNISHMENT

The American penal system as well as penology in the Western democracies is an outgrowth of the Quaker innovation of valuing the rehabilitation of criminals over their punishment. The earliest Quakers had been so often subject to arrest, imprisonment, and impoverishment in England that their successors were sensitive to how unjust a judicial system could be. They regarded capital punishment as "cruel and unusual."

In 1794, Pennsylvania abolished capital punishment for all crimes except murder in the first degree. However, colonial Quakers continued to impose harsh punishments for the sexual abuse of women. Today, Friends are unanimous in opposing capital punishment, a penalty the federal government and many states still assess but other Western democracies have abolished because it appears to sanction revenge.

FREEDOM, POWER, AND LIBERATION

Given their own history of persecution by government, Quakers were determined to ensure that politics be moral. Penn believed politics to be "a part of religion itself, a thing sacred in its institution and its end." Quakers were quick to oppose any government that was not fair in its application to all citizens.

As self-proclaimed "dissenters in their own land," they actually supported the founding of competing religious and political parties in Pennsylvania and elsewhere in the new nation. To safeguard freedom and encourage individual responsibility, they encouraged minimal government supported by minimal taxation. In 1692, for example, they rejected a proposed tax of a penny on a pound, equal to four-tenths of 1 percent of assessed wealth, as "a great tax" and a burden, depriving the citizenry of "liberties and properties."

In modern parlance, the early American Quakers might be styled as libertarians because they favored personal responsibility over regulation by government. Long before the American Revolution, William Penn caused the full text of the Magna Carta to be published in Philadelphia. Whereas many other Christians defined "freedom of conscience" as liberty to do only that which is right, Quakers held that it extended even to an individual's ideas that others believed to be wrong.

If that smacks of anarchy, consider that the Quakers believe in an inner light that enables every individual to distinguish between truth and error and that—if left free to do so—truth will inevitably overcome error. The Quakers demanded that government should not only be restrained from interfering with anyone's conscience but actually protect and promote freedom of dissent.

Based on these notions of justice, the Pennsylvania Quakers, even before the American Revolution, ensured citizens the right to trial by a jury of peers, a speedy trial, and taxation only by consent of the governed. To ensure that taxation was fair, all tax laws expired automatically after just one year and had to be restored if still justified.

HOW QUAKER VALUES INFUSED THE CONSTITUTION

The first ten amendments to the U.S. Constitution, known collectively as the Bill of Rights, were adopted in 1791 after the model of the Constitution of Quaker-led Rhode Island. The same values had been protected in colonial Quaker Pennsylvania.

They provided for the following:

1. *Congress shall make no law respecting an establishment of religion, or prohibiting the free exercise thereof; or abridging the freedom of speech or the press; or the right of the people peaceably to assemble, and to petition the government for a redress of grievances.* All of these rights were protected for all citizens in Quaker Pennsylvania and other Quaker-dominated colonies prior to the formation of the United States. Formerly, Quakers had sorely suffered from the absence of such freedoms in England. Note the emphasis on *peaceable* assembly. In England, Quakers had been arrested and imprisoned for worshipping together. It's worth noting that some of the individual states retained established churches for a time after the Constitution was adopted. Quaker-dominated states, however, had respected freedom of religion for all citizens from the outset.

2. *A well-regulated militia being necessary to the security of a free State, the right of the people to keep and bear arms shall not be infringed.* Quakers opposed violence and a standing army but supported the right of citizens to defend themselves.

3. *No soldier shall, in time of peace, be quartered in any house without the consent of the owner, nor in time of war, but in a manner to be prescribed by law.*

4. *The right of the people to be secure in their persons, houses, papers, and effects, against unreasonable searches and seizures, shall not be violated, and no warrants shall issue but upon probable cause, supported by oath or affirmation, and particularly describing the place to be searched, and the persons or things to be seized.* Both amendments extend to all Americans the right to personal privacy and security of property already guaranteed by the Quaker-dominated colonies. Note that an "affirmation" may now substitute for the oaths that Quakers, on principle, refused to take.

5. *No person shall be held to answer for a capital, of otherwise infamous, crime, unless on a presentment or indictment of a grand jury, except in cases arising in the land or naval forces, or in the militia, when in actual service in time of war or public danger; nor shall any person be subject for the same offense to be twice put in jeopardy of life or limb; nor shall be compelled in any criminal case to be a witness against himself, nor be*

deprived of life, liberty or property, without due process of law; nor shall private property be taken for public use without just compensation. This amendment extended to all Americans the Quaker-established assurance of trial by jury of one's peers and protection against double jeopardy and self-incrimination as well as guaranteeing compensation for private property seized by government.

6. *In all criminal prosecutions, the accused shall enjoy the right to a speedy and public trial, by an impartial jury of the State and district wherein the crime shall have been committed, which district shall have been previously ascertained by law, and to be informed of the nature and cause of the accusation; to be confronted by the witnesses against him; to have compulsory process for obtaining witnesses in his favor, and to have the assistance of counsel for his defense.* Here again is reflected the Quaker assurance of impartiality and speedy justice. Note as well how it reflects the Quaker reverence for truth telling.

7. *In suits at common law, where the value in controversy shall exceed twenty dollars, the right of trial by jury shall be preserved, and no fact tried by a jury shall be otherwise re-examined in any court of the United States, than according to the rules of common law.* Twenty dollars isn't what it used to be in 1791, but here again is repeated the Quaker conviction that no case is so negligible that a citizen can be deprived of his right to a trial by a jury of his peers.

8. *Excessive bail shall not be required, nor excessive fines imposed, nor cruel and unusual punishments inflicted.* Quakers regarded excessive fines as inimical to an egalitarian society, biased against those least able to pay. Friends considered capital punishment to be "cruel and unusual" but failed to persuade all the states of the new nation of their interpretation.

9. *The enumeration in the Constitution of certain rights shall not be construed to deny or disparage others retained by the people.*

10. *The powers not delegated to the United States by the Constitution, nor prohibited by it to the States, are reserved to the States respectively, or to the people.* The Quaker sense of these texts is that individual rights are not given by government to citizens but that rights inhere in each individual and must be respected by government and society. Moreover, the Quaker belief in continuing revelation is here implicit: as the nation's conscience comes to grasp that other individual rights must also be protected, the Consti-

tution can and should be amended. Over time, as we know, Americans' consciences would also recognize that women and the races had equal rights as citizens.

PERSONAL FREEDOM

Quakers were quicker than other colonials to condemn slavery as contrary to their beliefs in equality and freedom of conscience. In 1712 the Pennsylvania legislature forbade the further importation of slaves into the colony, but the measure was countermanded by the English Crown. Still, slave-owning Friends in Pennsylvania declined from 70 percent before 1705 to only 10 percent after 1756. In 1758 the Philadelphia Yearly Meeting unanimously rejected "importing, buying, selling, or keeping slaves for term of life." As Quakers freed their slaves, they continued to provide for their welfare.

"The history of the early abolitionist movement," Arthur Zilversmit notes, "is essentially the record of Quaker antislavery activities." More about that in our final chapter.

★ ★ ★

If Quakers did not quite "invent" America, they contributed more than any other group to the founding ideals that sustain our national life. And they continue to define the American character—egalitarian, fair, peace loving, tolerant, charitable, responsible, plainspoken, and honest. For a people that reject preaching and proselytizing, Quakers have long since converted America to their way of thinking.

To the Quaker way of thinking, all peoples, whatever their faith or lack thereof, are Friends because there is that of God in everyone. Just as orphans are impelled to search for their birth parents, all Americans can profit from seeking out the parentage of the beliefs we take for granted as our legacy. That is what the following chapters aim to do.

· 2 ·

Faith versus Feeling

This is my commandment: that you love each other
as I have loved you. . . . I call you friends. . . .

—John 15:12, 15

Now I was come up in spirit . . . into the Paradise of God.

—George Fox

Ever since the Age of Enlightenment, people of faith have been suspected of being either superstitious, sentimental, or both. Granted, religious faith is not something anyone acquires solely by cold reason, but that does not make it *un*reasonable to believe in something greater than our own selves.

To give its critics their due, religious faith in practice is too often merely emotional, inadequately exposed to the kind of thought taking that we apply to practical matters, like choosing a career or purchasing a car.

But it is wrongheaded to discount our affections altogether in making life choices. For example, I did not choose to marry a particular woman for life because she met the stringent requirements of a laboratory experiment. Rather, I fell in love with her and reasoned that the love she aroused in me was merited by her character.

To marry is therefore an act of faith but a reasonable one. So is the choice of having children. If those faiths fail in practice, it is not because we relied on our emotions but because either our judgment was flawed or the persons involved failed to measure up to reasonable expectations.

Theologians whom I respect believe that the existence of God can be proved by reason alone. If so, it is not the God of love proclaimed by Jesus of Nazareth (or Abraham or Mohammed) but rather a machine-like Prime Mover or First Cause—a divine clock maker who merely ensures the regularity of the universe.

A religious faith deserving of the name cannot be the product of our reason alone. We do not create God by believing in him; he creates us to love us. Moreover, he is not just the object of our faith but its source. All Christians agree that faith is a gift and that God is the sole giver. The manner by which each of us comes to faith varies: some of us more by thinking, others by feeling.

As they do everything else, Quakers tend to simplify the subject of faith. William Penn, the Quaker founder of Pennsylvania, defined religion as "nothing else but the love of God and man." The twentieth-century Quaker philosopher Rufus Jones simply acknowledged that "the springs of religion lie deep down in the elemental nature of human life itself." The poet T. S. Eliot echoed the Quakers, insisting that mere knowledge is an inadequate basis for a life of faith: "We know too much," he argued, "and are convinced of too little."

Contemporary Quakers shrink from giving the appearance of being cocksure in their faith. Many Friends in my experience prefer to characterize themselves instead as lifelong "seekers" because that seems to be less prideful. Because they believe in continuing revelation, they feel there's ever more to learn and that their faith at any one time in their lives is less than complete.

Quakers believe that people's sense of the sacred is unavoidable, even palpable, because the creator inheres in every individual. In that sense, everyone is religious. But as we know, many notional believers are content to go through the motions of religious practice without conviction or conversion and without love of God and service to others. Taking note of that fact, Oscar Wilde charged that "religion is the fashionable substitute for belief." People can acknowledge religion yet remain indifferent to it. Quakers hold that it is not enough to merely possess faith; one must also be faithful to one's beliefs. That requires acting on them.

Still, many Quakers are shy of proclaiming their convincement and attempting to articulate their faith as Friends. Quakers can be a little like "Doubting Thomas," the apostle who was skeptical of Jesus' Resurrection until the risen Christ appeared before him, and the apostle apologized: "Lord, I believe; help my unbelief." Like most of us, Thomas already had faith; he just needed to *grow* into it.

Nearly half of American Protestants refer to themselves as "born again," based on an *experience* in their adolescent or adult lives that persuaded them that they are saved through Christ. That kind of convincement makes no room for doubt. The evangelical Christian believes that his or her human nature already has been utterly *transformed* by grace, not just assisted by it.

George Fox, the founder of the Quaker movement, had such an experience. Here is how he described it:

> Now I was come up in spirit, through the flaming sword, into the paradise of God. All things were new, and all the creation gave another smell unto me than before, beyond what words can utter. I knew nothing but pureness, innocency, and righteousness, being renewed up into the image of God by Christ Jesus, so that I was come up into the state of Adam, which he was in before he fell.

Evangelical Christians are prone to ask perfect strangers, "Are you saved?" If your experience is anything like Fox's, you will be persuaded that you are destined to live forever with God and would want others to be.

However, despite the example of Fox's ecstatic conversion, I have yet to have a Friend approach me to ask if I have been saved. If salvation rests wholly on having such a life-altering experience, I would have to say no. Most Quakers make do with much less. Faith coexists with doubt and is tested by it.

Moreover, Friends hold that salvation is not a once-and-for-all-time guaranteed matter; rather, we all must work out our salvation day by day with the help of God's grace. That is why Quaker testimony shuns words in favor of deeds.

To be sure, faith for most believers (Quakers included) is more a matter of habit than emotional experience. People profess a faith they may neither feel nor articulate but maintain it nonetheless because they rest it on God's promise. For them, faith is faithfulness, and salvation is something they invest in every day of their lives by dealing faithfully with God and one another.

At the same time as they rely on God's forgiveness, Friends acknowledge the inherent contradictions in human nature. They consider themselves to be religious not because they are good but because they believe. They may not always sense the indwelling Spirit but are confident in praying to a God "out there." They may only seldom experience the "living Christ" but acknowledge the Jesus who lived and died for them 2,000 years ago.

If Quakers are not noisily cocksure, they are nevertheless quietly upbeat, neither obsessed by sin and salvation (as some evangelicals are) nor overly concerned with the doctrinal content of their faith (as many mainstream Christians are). Rather than righteousness and creeds, Friends prefer the love of God and the service of man as the basis of their faith lives. They seek to exemplify their faith by the way they conduct themselves. Although they acknowledge human frailty, they do not consider human nature to be corrupt. If pressed, Quakers suspect that people, although born imperfect, are yet perfectible this side of eternity.

Quakers divert their attention from sin and dogma to concentrate on the fundamentals of faithful living. When combined with a shrugging off of nonessentials in worship, the effect is liberating. When my wife and I first encountered Quakers, I wondered aloud how they could be sure their inspiration was from God and not from their own selfish imagination. A young "elder" replied in the words of the Gospel: "By their fruits you shall know them." In short, he explained, judge Friends not by what they merely say but by what they do.

There is a tendency among Friends to think the best of people. This is a virtue but, taken to an extreme, can incline them to believe that human nature is essentially innocent—despite all the evidence to the contrary. Being unusually kind people themselves, they would like to believe (quite innocently) that everyone else, down deep, is nice as well and that what religion has traditionally called sin is only culturally or psychologically aggravated misbehavior. In any case, Quakers are persuaded that peace is possible, that conflicts can be resolved, and that violence can be avoided. As we will see, they have good reason to believe they are correct in this.

Still, Friends are not naive. Many disagree with Robert Browning's assurance that because God's in his heaven, all is well with the world. The case for human innocence suffers a twofold failure: that people are inclined to turn a blind eye to their own sins and to sugarcoat the world's evils.

George Fox and the earliest generations of Quakers succeeded in being activists and pacifists at the same time. Not all Quakers are doctrinaire pacifists, but all abhor violence and seek to resolve human conflict peacefully. They do not confuse pacifism with passivity, which is to do nothing.

Just because Quaker faith is simple and welcomes inspiration does not make it fuzzy. Years ago, while preparing Quaker children to join their parents and other adults in silent worship, I cautioned the youngsters not to expect much in the way of inspiration but simply to bring the concerns of their everyday lives to worship so they might better be able to act out their faith as Friends.

Of course, well-meaning people can unwittingly substitute emotion and sentiment for faith and action, resulting in an artificial religion that is simply self-serving. In fact, many American Christians combine New Age thinking with conventional religious practices because New Age is so upbeat. Visit any large bookstore, and you will find a section devoted to "New Age" that rivals the space accorded to religion.

Unlike traditional religious faith, New Age is more a matter of personal attitude than creed or practice. It seeks nothing more than the development of one's own human potential. How that is achieved—be it by meditation, exercise, psychology, or herbal remedies—is not important, nor do New Agers argue about what form personal fulfillment takes. Serenity, sex, money, power: all are equally valid in the New Age lexicon.

Because they welcome personal inspiration, some Quakers find New Age thinking attractive, until they realize that New Age dispenses altogether with any God other than oneself. New Age actress Shirley Maclaine explains that, once one grasps that "you are God, you can create your own reality." New Age optimism has no more room for sin or grace than for God—only for failure or success in living up to one's self-gratification and self-esteem.

Still, the helpful lesson in New Age thinking is utter responsibility for oneself, and that is something Quakers believe in. Considerably less attractive is the absence of any imperative in New Age to be responsible for one another, which is also a Quaker imperative.

According to the New Age canon, if your reality is unsatisfactory, there is no one to blame but yourself. If you are poor or sick or unattractive, it is your own fault, and no one is required to come to aid you in your distress.

The similarities of New Age and Quakerism are obvious, but so are the differences. Friends seek self-fulfillment in the Light but recognize that others are in need and that Friends are duty bound to help them. Friends balance their self-concern with concern for others. The needs of the community are equally important to meet as are those of the individual.

Recent Gallup polls reveal that the overwhelming majority of Americans believe in developing their religious beliefs independent of organized religion. Unfortunately, in practice, the resulting product is a fuzzy, fragile do-it-yourself faith that lacks conviction. Half a century ago, sociologist Will Herberg lamented that

> the religiousness characteristic of America today is very often a religiousness without religion, a religiousness without almost any kind of context or none, a way of sociability or "belonging" rather than a way of reorienting life to God . . . a religiousness without serious commitment, without real conviction, without genuine existential decision.

It is harder for Quakers than for many other Christians to fall into these traps since Friends are judged by their actions.

Traditional Christianity holds that everything necessary for one's salvation has already been revealed in Scripture and that God's requirements are equivalent for everyone, without exception. That doesn't necessarily preclude continuing revelation by way of personal inspiration, but it does acknowledge it to be unnecessary.

Quakers, who trust in continuing revelation, can be tempted to treasure as the most important truth what they experience personally and privately. When feeling becomes fundamental, thinking takes second place because it is only human, whereas inspiration is divine. George Fox, trusting in the light within him, distrusted theological disputation. His suspicions of scholarship actually delayed the founding of Durham University—England's most prominent theological school—for two centuries on the grounds that mere human learning is inadequate.

But to his everlasting credit, Fox resisted turning the Quakers into a cult with himself as its guru saint. The founder was passionate but sensible. When some early Quakers literally quaked and foamed at the mouth under the influence of inspiration, Fox turned aside, impressed only with the inspiration, not its physical manifestations. He drew the line between the experience of God within us and those Quakers, like James Nayler, who identified themselves with the God within.

Fox acknowledged that he did not always understand the promptings of the Spirit, and he admitted that his own inspirations were often commonplace and uninformative—not great new revelations but just better understandings of things he already believed.

Because of the Quaker preference for inspiration over theological disputation, the first generations of Quakers produced but one theologian: Robert Barclay. His book *An Apology for the True Christian Divinity* set forth fifteen propositions. Fourteen of them proposed what is either false or unnecessary in the beliefs and practices of the churches of his day. Only one explained the beliefs of Quakers: the doctrine of the inner light.

Barclay argued that inspiration is superior to tradition, Scripture, and reason alike—indeed, that Scripture ranks only as a "secondary rule" of living—but held the revelation contained in the Bible to be identical to the revelation given to Quakers, whom he called Children of the Light. He pronounced that revelation to be self-evident:

> The Divine revelation and inward illumination is that which is evident and clear of itself; forcing, by its own evidence and clearness, the well-disposed understanding to assent, irresistibly moving the same thereunto . . .

So, Barclay taught, the truth of inspiration is available to all persons and self-evident to anyone who is "well disposed" to receive it. Fox for one, was clearly well disposed. He did not theorize about the Inner Light but walked in it and was not satisfied until he saw others walking in it with him. It was not the *novelty* of his inspirations that impressed him as much as the depth of the experience. He attempted neither to replace Scripture nor to add to it but only to better sense its meaning and put it into practice in his life.

On occasion, Fox's inspiration puzzled even himself. One day, approaching Lichfield, the sight of the church's three spires "struck at his life." Leaving his shoes with shepherds, he ran miles into town barefoot, crying, "Woe to the city of Lichfield!" When he returned to reclaim his shoes, Fox said, "The fire of the Lord was so in my feet and all over me that I did not matter to put them on . . . till I felt a freedom of the Lord to do so." He never could explain why he had acted in such a way. Later, commentators speculated that Fox had been told as a boy that the last executions for Christian heresy had taken place at Lichfield a dozen years before he was born.

Contemporary Quakers no longer proselytize, either barefoot or well shod. Ronald Knox, the former Catholic chaplain at Oxford and a scholar of the early Quakers, wrote of them,

> What survived, as we know, was a religious coterie rather than a sect; a band of well-to-do reformers, distinguished by their wide influence and active benevolence, but numbering only a handful of adherents among the multitudes on whom they had compassion.

Knox reflected that a mere "coterie" of Friends was not at all what Fox had in mind when he preached to anyone who would listen to him. Fox meant to convert the entire world to the Light and devoted the rest of his life to doing so.

To an extraordinary extent, he succeeded, and the America in which we now live incorporates his values and his vision.

• 3 •

The Meaning of the Light

And God said, Let there be light, and there was light . . .

—Genesis 1:3

$\mathcal{Q}$uakers routinely refer to an Inner Light shared by every person. Friends explain their prayers for others as "holding them in the Light." Of course, they don't pretend to possess a patent or copyright on illumination, but the doctrine of the Inner Light underlies their belief in God's continuing revelation of himself through personal inspiration.

In the Bible the symbol of light literally leads the Old Testament account of Creation, and light figures just as prominently in the New Testament in the Prologue to the Gospel according to St. John.

Here is the familiar account of Creation in the Book of Genesis:

> In the beginning God created the heaven and the earth. And the earth was without form, and void; and darkness was upon the face of the deep. And the spirit of God moved upon the face of the waters. And God said, "Let there be light": and there was light. And God saw the light, that it was good . . . (Genesis 1:1–3)

The very act of creation is the passing from darkness into light. As we know, the existence of life itself depends on the availability of light. Nothing grows in the dark. We need light to find our way in the darkness.

In the New Testament, St. John refers to the Creation in a different way but again employs the imagery of light:

> In the Beginning was the Word, and the Word was with God, and the Word was God. . . . In him was life; and the life was the light of

27

men. And the light shineth in the darkness; and the darkness com-
prehended it not. There was a man sent from God, whose name was
John. The same came for a witness, to bear witness of the Light, that
all men through him might believe. He was not that Light, but was
sent to bear witness of that Light. That was the true Light, which
lighteneth every man that cometh into the world. . . . (John 1:1–10)

So light is God's creation that makes it possible for us to see and discern
and for things to grow, thrive, and mature. In the New Testament, light
is personified. The Creator enters human history in the person of Jesus
of Nazareth to share our humanity and enlighten. As the evangelist acknowledges, it is possible to reject that light.

There are additional references to light in the New Testament. In
the first scene Jesus, risen from the dead, has returned to his Father after
forty days, but not before promising to send his Spirit to take his place
among his followers. The apostles are gathered in Jerusalem when

> Before their eyes appeared tongues like flames, which separated off
> and settled upon each one of them. They were all filled with the
> Holy Spirit and began to speak in different languages as the Spirit
> gave them power to proclaim the message . . . (Acts 2:3–4)

Here, light possessed the power to both inspire and reveal. Also in the
Acts of the Apostles is the account of how Saul, the persecutor of Christians, was literally blinded by the Light and plunged into darkness:

> As he neared Damascus, a light from the sky suddenly blazed around
> him, and he fell to the ground. Then he heard a voice speaking to
> him: "Saul, Saul, why are you persecuting me?" "Who are you,
> Lord?" he asked. "I am Jesus whom you are persecuting" was the re-
> ply. . . . Saul got up from the ground, but when he opened his eyes
> he could see nothing and he remained sightless for three days. . . .
> When Ananias went to Saul, he said: "Saul, brother, the Lord has sent
> me—Jesus who appeared to you on your journey here—so that you
> may recover your sight, and be filled with the Holy Spirit." Immedi-
> ately something like scales fell from Saul's eyes, and he could see
> again. . . . (Acts 9:3–9, 17–18).

Ironically, Saul, the Christians' persecutor, previously blind *to* the Light,
is now blinded *by* it. Once converted to Christ by his experience, he not
only regains his sight but now sees everything in a entirely different light.

Fast-forward to George Fox. Fox believed that the Christ offered by the church in his time was too small and was being made the prisoner of Scripture rather than our liberator. In the words of the contemporary Quaker historian John Punshon, Fox proclaimed,

> For those who repented . . . Christ was already here and was to be found within. To find him, one condition was necessary . . . it was to exercise true repentance, to turn to the living Christ within, by whom alone the reality of other discoveries would be revealed.

Fox appropriated the figure of light to express this inward reality. Again, John Punshon:

> The light is that of God within you, and is not your conscience or intellect, though it may work through them. It is active and loving. It will show you your sins. It carries power and will enable you to overcome them. It is in all people, and if listened to will lead its hearers into unity with one another. It guides, warns, encourages, speaks, chastens, cares. It is something on which you may place total reliance.

What the light first revealed was one's sins. To be convinced meant to be convinced of your sin in the sense of being "convicted" of one's misdeeds and shortcomings. So conversion began unpleasantly, as it did for Saul on the road to Damascus. It was shock therapy, eliciting remorse and requiring radical rehabilitation. The early Friends earned the name Quakers because they literally trembled—not in fear but in the joyous feeling of release from sin and the power of God to forgive it.

As Catholics believe in Christ's real presence in the consecrated bread and wine, Quakers find him in the Light.

In the Light, Jesus Christ spoke to Fox's condition when all his hopes in worldly things had disappeared.

What this inferred was that God's revelation did not end with the last page of the Bible but continues in the Light. God is not the prisoner of either Scripture or his church but free to speak and inspire through his Spirit.

That belief is not confined to Quakers. One frigid January night in 2002, Ron Buford, a marketing executive, lay sleepless in his Cleveland home, his mind occupied with slogans, seeking inspiration for his clients' commercial advertising campaigns. As he later recalled, he sat bold upright with the sudden inspiration that God was speaking.

Not that God was singling him out for a special revelation but only that "God is still speaking" to everyone if they will only listen. Buford sold his slogan to the 1.4-million-member United Church of Christ, which earmarked $30 million for a commercial television campaign that began in late 2004 with the aim of attracting unchurched Americans to that denomination.

Mainstream Christianity leans to the opinion that God's revelation to humankind is encompassed in the Old and New Testaments and was completed in the century following the death and resurrection of Jesus. However, agreement on which books deserved to be included in the Bible was not reached until the fourth century. Until then, there was plenty of competition among writings that claimed to be the inspired word of God.

In any case, scriptural revelation is not exhaustive. If we were restricted to what we can find in the Bible, we would note that Jesus told slaves to obey their masters and soldiers to obey their officers. Nor, for example, did he say anything about same-sex relations that might help his church today to reach agreement. As it was, it took Christendom nineteen centuries to come to the conclusion that human slavery is immoral. To this day, pacifists look not to the Bible but to Jesus' own example of nonresistance to support their condemnation of violence.

Historically, the earliest of Christian heresies was Gnosticism, which held that only the elect were privy to God's light. That popular heresy reveled in making God's revelation mysterious and Christianity into an exclusive club. Echoes of Gnosticism persist in the teaching of Nostradamus. Judaism has its counterpart in Kabalah. Scientology thrives on being esoteric. New Age religion relies on an inner inspiration that transforms the believer into his or her own God. All of these are exclusive clubs with secret revelations.

Whereas Fox insisted that the inner light shines on everyone without exception. As Ronald Knox, the late Catholic chaplain of Oxford University, explained, "To live by the inner light is in some sense to be divinized, to realize the dwelling of God's Spirit in us . . ." The early Quakers were steeped in Scripture, so much so that they were not just listening to the Bible but living in it. Fox taught that if one adopts the inner light as one's rule of faith, it supersedes Scripture and (if need be) overrides the authority of written revelation.

Fortunately, the church and Scripture stand as bulwarks against personal fantasies posing as messages from God and against fellowships that claim to possess the exclusive key to the creator. Individual Quakers might be tempted to cling to their own personal inspirations, thereby separating them from other Friends, but there has always been a discipline of faith and practice within the Society of Friends that has deterred them from becoming eccentric and arrogant.

Friends revere Scripture but do not worship it. To do so would be a sin of idolatry. Rather, they worship a living, personal God—creator and redeemer, alpha and omega, and every creature's certain hope. For Friends, God seeking is unnecessary because God has already sought us and found us, becoming one of us in the person of Jesus of Nazareth. All one needs to do is to allow the Light to enter and enlighten us.

Researcher Dr. Melvin Morse specializes in accounts of near-death experiences. He claims that millions of people around the world have penetrated the frontier between life and death, time and eternity. Typically, they report the experience of having been "embraced by the light" before returning to everyday life transformed into fearless and loving people.

Was it God they saw in the light? Few who have ventured to the frontier between life and death attempt to analyze their experience because they find it incomparable. When asked about the light she had seen, one woman told Dr. Morse, "It wasn't God, but it wasn't *not* God."

By contrast, St. Paul did not hesitate to identify the light. God's Holy Spirit, he reported, illumined "things which eye saw not, and ear heard not, and which entered not into the heart of man, whatsoever things God has prepared for them that love him." The same light, Paul insisted, was available to everyone.

From time immemorial, the human journey from ignorance and fear to knowledge and peace has been characterized as one from darkness into light. The Israelites of Jesus' time believed that, after death, their souls would inhabit a dark waiting place they called Sheol, awaiting deliverance into light.

In his allegory *The Divine Comedy*, Dante described the soul's ascent from hell's darkness to heaven's light. For the poet it was a personal pilgrimage. "Midway this way of life we're bound upon," he wrote, "I awoke to find myself in a dark wood, where the right road was wholly lost and gone."

Darkness signifies not only ignorance and confusion but also doubt and the lack of a sense of direction. Job in his misery lacked the light to see God: "I hoped for happiness, but sorrow came; I looked for light, but there was darkness."

But Friends hold that God himself operates in the light. Of God, Job complained, "If I go to the east he is not there; or to the west, I still cannot see him. If I seek him in the north, he is not to be found, invisible as ever if I turn to the south. And yet he knows every step I take!"

Those who despair of faith mourn the loss of light. The unbelieving poet Matthew Arnold lamented that

> The sea of faith
> Was once, too, at the full, and round earth's shore
> Lay like the folds of a bright girdle furl'd.

But Arnold remarked about his own unbelieving world,

> So various, so beautiful, so new,
> Hath really neither joy, nor love, nor light,
> Nor certitude, nor peace, nor help for pain;
> And we are here on a darkling plain
> Swept with confused alarms of struggle and flight,
> Where ignorant armies clash by night.

The novelist William Styron, suffering clinical depression, characterized his illness as the disappearance of faith and the waning of the light: "In depression this faith in deliverance, in ultimate restoration, is absent. It is hopelessness even more than pain that crushes the soul."

Yet people of faith insist that God can manifest himself even in the darkness. T. S. Eliot compared the experience to that of a theatergoer: "I said to my soul, be still, and let the dark come upon you / Which shall be the darkness of God. As, in a theater, / The lights are extinguished, for the scene to be changed . . . / So the darkness shall be the light. . . ."

St. John of the Cross agreed with Dante that the journey to enlightenment must proceed through darkness:

> The journey is a dark night because the individual must not cling to any worldly possessions. This is a night for the senses because the road one travels is faith. And for the intellect this is like a dark night because the point of arrival is God, a dark night to us in this life. . . . Faith lies beyond all understanding, taste, feeling, and imagination that one has. . . . The soul must journey to God by knowing God through what God is not, rather than by knowing what God is.

That great mystic did not mean to deter others from seeking enlightenment but only to accept that God, the author of light, does not fit into human categories. The creator is, by his own revelation, our father, but only by human analogy. Human preconceptions only limit and misrepresent God.

The Psalmist cried to God "in the night" and complained that "all that I know is the dark." Yet he persisted in faith, seeking the light. Alfred, Lord Tennyson, reconciled himself to the fact that "There lives more faith in honest doubt, / Believe me, than in half the creeds."

Or, perhaps, in *all* of them. Quakers, relying on continuing revelation, refuse to reduce their faith to mere words or to ancient history. God's light, Friends attest, emanates from the creator, not from the printed page or the pulpit.

The late English Cardinal Basil Hume, a Benedictine monk, meditated about the mystery of love between creator and creature, likening it to a cloud that hovers between them:

> From time to time that cloud of unknowing is pierced by a shaft of light which tells us something about God, though we do not see or touch him directly. . . . There are times when any one of us may experience terrible desolation. Then it helps to recall those other days when we caught, albeit "in a glass darkly," a glimpse of him. Perhaps it was in beauty, seen or heard, or being in the presence of a loved one—an icon of his loveableness.

The great Christian apologist C. S. Lewis was fond of noting that people are blinded by looking directly at the sun but that it is only by the sun's reflected light that we are permitted to see anything at all.

My wife likens the grappling of faith and doubt to Jacob wrestling with the angel. Gerard Manley Hopkins suggested that the believer is actually wrestling with God himself: "Of now done darkness I wretch lay wrestling with (my God!) my God."

The Psalmist expressed the same notion when he affirmed that "the Lord is my shepherd," confident that "even were I to walk in a ravine as dark as death I should fear no evil, for you are at my side."

Teresa of Avila, the Spanish mystic, explained,

> God removes the scales from the eyes and lets the soul see and understand something of the grace received in a strange and wonderful

way . . .by intellectual vision . . . preceded by an illumination which shines on the spirit like a most dazzling cloud of light. . . . So what once was a doctrine of faith, the soul now understands by sight. . . .

In any event, the passing from darkness to light is not an intellectual search. Faith is a gift, not a reward or an accomplishment. Faith actually *precedes* comprehension and is a precondition for understanding. As St. Anselm affirmed of himself, "I do not seek to understand in order that I may believe, but I believe in order that I may understand."

Poets and mystics enjoy an advantage over the rest of us in articulating their experience of God. But there is no reason to believe that God favors them over those of us with less imagination. In any event, it is far more important that God pay attention to us than that we comprehend him. As the Psalmist acknowledges,

> You know when I sit, when I rise
> You understand my thoughts from afar . . .
> Where shall I go to escape your spirit?
> Where shall I flee from your presence? . . .
> I will say, "Let the darkness cover me,
> And the night wrap itself around me,"
> Even darkness to you is not dark,
> And night is as clear as the day.

When my wife's father died, there were no clergy to offer prayers at his internment, so members of the family provided prayers in faith, hope, and remembrance. I borrowed some lines from *Adonais*, Shelley's elegy on the death of Keats. Here is the poet's grasp of the light:

> Heaven's light forever shines, Earth's shadows fly;
> Life, like a dome of many-colored glass,
> Stains the white radiance of eternity . . .
> That Light whose smile enkindles the Universe,
> That Beauty in which all things work and move,
> That Benediction which the eclipsing Curse
> Of birth can quench not, that sustaining Love
> Which through the web of being blindly wove
> By man and beast and earth and air and sea,
> Burns bright or dim, as each are mirrors of
> The fire for which all thirst . . .

Shelley concludes with confidence that his friend now lives in eternal light. It is a convincement shared by all Friends:

> . . . burning through the inmost veil of Heaven,
> Adonais, like a star,
> Beacons from the abode where the Eternal are.

• 4 •

The Significance of Jesus

I myself am the way, and the truth, and the life.

—John 14:6

$\mathcal{A}$t burgeoning Patrick Henry College, just outside the nation's capital, all students applying for admission must answer the question, "What is your personal relationship with Jesus?"

That is not a question that Quakers often pose to themselves or to one another. When Friends on the highway see a bumper sticker that reads, "Honk if you love Jesus!" they pass by silently because it is their peculiar tradition to display reverence through silence.

Moreover, a small minority of Quakers manage to resist classification as Christians. In our Virginia meeting, we have a sprinkling of Jews, Muslims, and Buddhists, and it's fair to say that there are more undefined "seekers" in our company than convinced members who look solely to Christ. Many contemporary Friends of my acquaintance are more comfortable considering Quakerism to be a movement rather than a sect.

Then again, there are Quakers and there are Quakers. The current total of 206,000 American Friends are roughly divided between those in the West and Midwest, who are affiliated with Friends United, whose worship incorporates much of what you would find in many Protestant churches. They are all Christians.

Whereas those Quakers in the eastern United States, who are affiliated with Friends General Conference, hew to "unprogrammed" worship, which is to say communal silence. They are more accommodating of persons raised in other faith traditions. Still, all Quakers revere their Christian heritage and look to Jesus of Nazareth as their inspiration. I would venture to guess that most of us would feel awkward applying to Patrick Henry College.

At age seventeen, I could not have written an essay on a college application describing my personal relationship with Jesus—not because I was indifferent or ignorant but because I did not have the "born-again" experience claimed by half of Protestant Christians in America. I was a cradle Christian and have ever since taken for granted my relationship with Jesus as something he established. I have never been comfortable with the notion that Jesus belongs to me but rather that I belong to him.

C. S. Lewis wrote, "The real question is not what we are to make of Jesus, but what is he to make of us?" When my wife and I were but fledgling Quakers, our clerk asked us what tests a Friend's faith. Becky replied correctly that it is the transformation faith brings about in us. G. K. Chesterton suggested something similar when he noted that "Christianity has not been tried and found wanting; it has been found to be difficult and has yet to be tried."

The pacifist Phillip Berrigan, long imprisoned for acting out his faith, declared, "I am a Catholic *trying* to be a Christian." Quakers attempt the same transformation of their lives by action.

Here we encounter some confusion. Almanacs and religious reference books tend not to classify Quakers as a Christian sect. Instead, they are placed at the undefined margin along with Universalists, Unitarians, and Mormons. An English friend of mine, the 1999 Swarthmore lecturer Alex Wildwood actually describes himself as an *ex*-Christian, still rebelling against the Christianity of his youth. He would prefer a Quaker faith that does not depend on Jesus.

In addition to the Jews, Muslims, Buddhists, and agnostics in our Quaker meeting, there are Friends who were raised in a variety of Christian denominations they left behind. One of our company characterizes most of us as "renegades." Considering this absence of uniformity, what significance can Jesus have for each and every Friend?

For starters:

- We measure time from Jesus' birth—a clear secular appreciation of his significance. The new millennium lacks meaning apart from him.
- Christians believe that Jesus inaugurated God's kingdom and that we live in a New Creation. That's clearly significant.

- Christians believe that Jesus accomplished what we cannot do for ourselves: to save us *from* ourselves and to save us *for* God. Whether or not individual Friends hold Jesus to be divine, he clearly showed us God in a way no one ever did before or has since. That, too, is significant.
- Christians believe that God's spirit dwells in us because of Jesus. Paul said, "I live: no, not I, but Christ lives in me" (Galatians 2:20). And Jesus himself said, "Wherever two or three are gathered together in my name, I am there with them" (Matthew 18:20).
- Jesus is clearly significant because he succeeded in turning society's values upside down and inside out. In place of power, pride, and wealth, he blessed the weak, the humble, and the poor. After Jesus, we cannot pass a homeless man or woman in the street without knowing that God loves that person *as much* as he loves us.
- Among religious leaders, Jesus is unique in his claim. Mohammed claimed only to be a prophet, the Buddha to have tasted enlightenment, Abraham and Moses to have been God's servants. Jesus alone professed to be both Son of Man and Son of God.
- Jesus is significant because he did not tell us much about himself except what was most important to us. Unlike other prominent persons, he wrote no self-serving autobiography. Still, we probably know more about Jesus than about any other person in antiquity.
- We certainly know what his followers believed about him, plus a remarkably consistent set of things he said and did in a relatively short period of his life. Not many historical characters have four parallel narrative accounts of their life and teaching, as we have in the Gospels.

Still we need to ask ourselves, Are those Gospels false to Jesus because they are not critical histories but testimonies of faith instead? For the sake of argument, let's pretend that they are only mythical accounts. But if they are, then the following holds:

- Their consistency is difficult to explain. How could so many mythmakers agree on the same story?

- It's clear that the writers and witnesses believed their own myths because they lived and died defending them.
- It's equally clear that their encounter with Jesus utterly transformed those simple and fickle men.

Biblical scholars in the "Jesus Seminar" question whether many of the statements in the Gospels attributed to Jesus really issued from his mouth. Let's concede that some of what we know about Jesus may be enhancement. But a myth is not a lie: it is only a truth that is not wholly literal.

Everyone believes in a myriad of myths. We believe in motherhood (despite the existence of bad mothers), in patriotism (despite traitors), and in love and happy endings (despite divorce and hatred).

A myth is the significance one attributes to things: an explanation rooted in reality, not just in imagination, often a moral. Christians, for example, don't say they *believe* Jesus; rather, they affirm that they believe *in* him, trusting him as a person.

Think back to those college applicants, each describing his and her personal relationship to Jesus. Just as St. Paul and St. John had different appreciations of Jesus, so will the students. But it is the *same* Jesus they are describing. Jesus does not change to suit what anyone happens to think about him.

Who is that Jesus? He is not someone that the earliest Christians first met in the Gospels; rather, they encountered him either in person or through witnesses. There were Christians long before the Gospels were written. In a sense, the Gospels are only afterthoughts, written for later generations after the eyewitnesses had passed from the scene. Paul's letters, which explain Jesus' significance, were written even *before* the first Gospel was circulated.

Significantly, the Gospels are anything but puff pieces. They are gritty stories of pain, disappointment, betrayal, and ultimate triumph. That Jesus' Apostles sometimes come off so badly in the Gospels actually speaks for their credibility. A Peter who denies Jesus and a Judas who betrays him are more believable than a thousand plaster saints.

Jesus was much more than he was esteemed by those closest to him. John's Jesus, for example, is the eternal divine expression of God ("In the beginning was the Word"), whereas St. Matthew begins his Gospel tracing Jesus' purely human antecedents.

What was he like? Lamentably, we have inherited a serene, sanitized Jesus, whereas the Gospel accounts depict a Jesus who was not at all serene but tired, hungry, sleep deprived, angry, disappointed, passionate, fearful, tempted, demanding—and sometimes seemingly indifferent. As for a sanitized Jesus, we can be confident that he didn't bathe as often as we do and that he didn't send his clothes to the cleaners. As to his appearance, in the Roman catacombs he is depicted as clean shaven. Later artists persuaded themselves that by giving him a beard he would look more distinguished.

Isaiah predicted this of the Messiah:

> His appearance was disfigured beyond that of any man, and his form marred beyond human likeness. . . . He had no beauty or majesty to attract us to him, nothing in his appearance that we should desire him. He was despised and rejected by men, a man of sorrows, and familiar with suffering. Like one from whom men hide their faces, he was despised . . . (Isaiah 53:3)

Contemporary theologian Phillip Yancey points to a legend dating from the second century that suggests Jesus may have been a hunchback. In medieval times it was widely believed that he was a leper.

Napoleon, no pious zealot, said this of Jesus:

> Everything in Christ astonishes me. His spirit overawes me, and his will confounds me. Between him and whoever else in the world, there is no possible term of comparison. He is truly a being by himself. . . . I search in vain in history to find the similar to Jesus Christ, or anything that can approach the gospel. Neither history, nor humanity, nor the ages, nor nature, offer me anything with which to compare it or to explain it. Here everything is extraordinary.

G. K. Chesterton, raised as a child to consider Jesus a cardboard caricature, was shocked as an adult to discover the real Jesus in the Gospels to be

> an extraordinary being with lips of thunder and acts of lurid decision, flinging down tables, casting out devils, passing with the wild secrecy of the wind from mountain isolation to a sort of dreadful demagogy; a being who often acted like an angry god—and always like a god.

On what do Friends agree about Jesus' significance? In his book *A Call to Be Vital*, the modern Quaker philosopher Rufus Jones called Jesus "the supreme revelation":

> He has formed for us our basic conceptions of the nature and character of God. Most of us think of God in terms of the God and Father of Jesus Christ. . . . Love *exists* only where it is incarnated in a person. . . . The greatest single fact of history is the breaking in of the Life of God through this unique Life. Here at last the Love of God found complete expression.

Jones held Jesus to be as significantly a revelation of who we are as he is a revelation of who God is. No one, he argues, knows what it means to be human until he has seen humanity "reinterpreted in Christ." Because of Jesus, "the life of God is no more remote from us than the ocean is to the fish that swim in it. Seeing Jesus we see what God is like."

After twenty centuries, Jones insists, we are even more persuaded than his contemporaries of Jesus' significance:

> We who have not seen with our eyes, or touched with our hands, have seen Christ's power in operation, and it is easier to believe in Christ now than when men saw him with their own eyes.

How Quakers Approach the Bible

The early Quakers were saturated in the Bible; but they did
not treat it as a document [to be worshipped], because they
felt they were part of it.

—Monsignor Ronald Knox

"HERE IS MY SECRET"

*W*hen she was politely asked by a visiting African chief to reveal the
formula for her successful sixty-seven-year reign over the British Empire,
Queen Victoria presented him with one of her bibles, declaring, "Here
is my secret!"

That was late in the nineteenth century. No doubt the queen was
unaware that, three centuries earlier, the great Protestant reformer Martin Luther had already disputed her claim. Luther argued that it is impossible "to rule a country, let alone the entire world, by the gospel."
"God," he said, "has placed human civil life under the dominion of natural reason, which has the ability to rule physical things," and concluded,
"We need not look to Scripture for advice."

Who was wiser: the queen or the churchman? Perhaps neither of
them. That would have been George Fox's judgment. The fate of nations is not in our hands in any case. What we do seek from revelation
is counsel on how to lead responsible, fulfilling lives—caring for those
entrusted to us and trusting God to keep his promises.

To give Victoria her due, the queen was persuaded that religious
faith is the secret to a meaningful life for herself as a grieving widow. For

this, she found the Bible to be a source of strength and inspiration. She believed hers to be a Christian nation.

The Bible can be a source of strength for everyone. But the challenge any inquirer faces at the outset is that the Bible is formidable in length (my copy runs to 1,862 pages of tiny type) and, to all appearances, lacks any coherent plot. Its text is complex, often arcane, and is filled with apparent contradictions. It needs not just translation but explanation.

Dictionaries and encyclopedias are alphabetized for easy reference, but we need a weighty Concordance to find our way through the Bible. So it's no wonder that people desperate for inspiration open the Bible at random and blindly lay their finger on a verse hoping it will impart the wisdom that will show them the way. Unfortunately, the Bible doesn't function very well as a Ouija board.

George Fox was a leader of the second wave of the Protestant Reformation. In the first wave of reform a century earlier, Martin Luther, John Calvin, John Knox, and others fixed on Scripture as the sure foundation of the Christian religion. In a sense, they substituted the Bible for the Church, but they were determined only to reform the church, not to dispense with it.

Fox, a century later, was far more radical. He appreciated the need for community and organized worship but not for the "steeple-houses," as he called church buildings, or for clergy and their preached lessons from Scripture. He also dispensed with the sacraments as repositories of grace dispensed by the church. It wasn't that Fox found sermons, liturgy, and visible sacraments to be of no value—he merely believed they were unnecessary and potentially a distraction from the true purpose of religion, which is to repent and love and serve God.

As for Scripture itself, Fox was steeped in it. Granted, he was no scholar. He had not studied Hebrew or Greek or even the Latin favored for the Catholic Bible. But he knew his Bible inside and out from the King James Version, and he believed in it. As a solitary young man tending the flocks, he ruminated on written revelation, making a lifelong home in it for himself and sharing it with everyone. Gerard Croese, the first Quaker historian, said the Bible "might be found in the mouth of George Fox."

Here is how Ronald Knox, the late Catholic chaplain of Oxford University, explains Fox's approach to the Scriptures:

Fox's attitude towards Scripture was that of the Anabaptists, not that of the Reformers. It is true that he was always ready and fully competent to chop texts with the higgling controversialists of his time; he could higgle with the best of them. If you questioned his repudiation of Baptism, he referred you to 1 Cor. 1:14: "I thank God that I baptized none of you," in flat defiance of the context, and went away satisfied.

Ronald Knox continues,

The truth is that if you adopt the inner light as your rule of faith, it necessarily supersedes and (if need be) overrides the authority of Scripture. Fox could not look upon the Bible as a collection of title-deeds, from which you derive your warrant for this or that; he was living in the Bible, his prophesies, his convincements, his power of reading hearts, were simply the continuation of what had been going on 16 centuries before.

Monsignor Knox concludes, "The early Quakers were saturated in the Bible; but they did not treat it as a document [to be worshipped], because they felt they were part of it."

The early Quakers had no doubt whatsoever that the Scriptures were inspired and that they were indeed God's revelation to humankind. But they insisted on a living Christ and a continuing revelation. Here is Fox's well-known description of his conversion:

Now I was come up in spirit, through the flaming sword, into the paradise of God. All things were new, and all the creation gave another smell unto me than before, beyond what words can utter. I knew nothing but pureness, innocency, and righteousness, being renewed up into the image of God by Christ Jesus, so that I was come up into the state of Adam, which he was in before he fell.

Note Fox's expression: "All things were new . . . beyond what words can utter." Biblical revelation, of course, is made up of words— and ancient words at that, whereas the Inner Light and the Indwelling Spirit are always fresh and new and present as the source of revelation for Fox and his followers.

Along with the Friends' attraction to simplicity, this helps explain why there is so little in the way of Quaker theology. Robert Barclay was the early exception, but his *Apology* is less an analysis of the Quaker faith than it is a criticism of what the churches of the time taught and did. Barclay agreed with Fox: if God's Spirit dwells in every man and woman, then all distinctions among us disappear, leaving only our willingness to listen to the Spirit and to open our eyes to the Inner Light. We have little need of academic theology because God makes himself known to each of us directly.

Recall that when my wife and I were fledgling Quakers, I asked our meeting's clerk how individual Friends could be sure that they were truly acting from inspiration rather than from selfish motives, wishful thinking, or a hidden agenda. In short, what test can be applied to ensure that, even if we are not completely right, that at least we are not acting wrongly?

The clerk had a ready answer, and it came not surprisingly from the Bible: "By their fruits you shall know them." Inspiration is internal and private, but our actions are public and open to scrutiny. Friends gather together seeking mutual inspiration, which helps us avoid eccentricity. We can judge the value of inspiration by what it leads us to do.

But Fox and the earliest Friends did not expect people to live passively in the Light as blank slates for the Spirit to write on. The Bible is the foundation of our faith. Even if it is not the last word in inspiration, it is the *first* word, and it is accessible to everyone, just as the Inner Light is.

Although two-thirds of Americans today believe the Bible answers all or most of the basic questions of life, 41 percent rarely or never read it. According to pollster George Gallup Jr., Americans are twice as biblically illiterate as we were at the beginning of the 1990s.

Friends tend to be friendly to the Bible, acknowledging that it "speaks to our condition." As Isaac Pennington argued, "It is the purpose of words to bring men to the knowledge of things beyond which words can utter."

Those who manage to read the Bible from cover to cover, beginning with Genesis, are like the weary adventurers who hike the length of the Appalachian Trail that extends from Georgia to Maine. At the conclusion all they can remember are the highlights of the journey. The rest is mindless drudgery.

Lamentably, Scripture is often wielded as a weapon of righteousness. Christians who oppose each other on public issues such as abortion, animal rights, homosexuality, capital punishment, and euthanasia quote passages from the Bible to justify their positions. No surprises here: it has long been conceded that the devil himself can quote Scripture to his advantage. There is so much in the Bible that it is easily quoted out of context and twisted to give the wrong signals.

Moreover, people probably demand too much of written revelation. The Bible was never intended to convey a comprehensive set of solutions to life's problems. In the final analysis, people are responsible for themselves. Consider this: if we relied only on the *letter* of Scripture, we might still tolerate slavery, and women would remain second-class citizens. Martin Luther surely had a point: conscience and reason are also our guides. And Fox was right to trust to the Inner Light.

For all the Bible's complexity, Moses managed to compress God's commandments to just ten, and Jesus further reduced them to two: to love God and to love our fellow creatures. In his Sermon on the Mount (Matthew 5–7), Jesus added refinements to those commandments, which, at first blush, confuse rather than clarify what God expects of us. Jesus exalted poverty (a condition every sensible person abhors), then transformed sorrow, suffering, and meekness from shortcomings into virtues. Moreover, he instructed us to love our enemies and pray for those who treat us badly. On encountering these precepts, we can be forgiven for not finding them to be clear formulas for confident living. They seem to make Christianity more of a burden than a consolation. Still, this is one of the means by which God chose to reveal himself to us.

Fortunately, biblical studies have developed such sophistication in the century recently ended that Jewish and Christian scholars of widely divergent traditions now enjoy many more points of agreement than disagreement. With only the occasional assistance of experts on obscure points, we can be the wiser, enjoying the confidence that comes from submitting our challenges and aspirations to God's written word.

Taken as a whole, the Bible is a compendium of God's dealing with his people, initially those who formed the tiny, fragile nations of Israel and Judea, then was expanded to include peoples of all nations. Strictly speaking, biblical revelation is not the story of individuals. If some characters in the Bible appear to be thinly drawn heroes and villains, it is because they enter the story only to illustrate a point or to act as a vehicle for God, who is the Bible's principal character. Some characters are legendary; indeed, some biblical critics consider them *only* legendary. Their role in the Old Testament is to illustrate the story of God entering history to heal the breach between creatures and creator. In the New Testament, God enters history in the person of his Son. Having initially created man in his image, God now makes himself in man's image.

Bible study has been facilitated in recent years by the personal computer, which can scan for word, subject, and phrase. At a book fair in London a few years ago, my wife and I witnessed bearded young Orthodox Jews at computer keyboards calling up God's revelation on-screen with just a few educated taps of their fingers.

For Bible hobbyists, it is tempting to become involved in trivia. But the Bible itself is anything but trivial; it is God's own word. Every now and then a publisher produces the Bible in a version meant to be read not as revelation but as literature. Such versions are tightly condensed and selective to keep them interesting and undemanding. By contrast, the real Bible is often tedious but always insistent. It is a book meant not just to be read but to be followed.

Not surprisingly, the Bible is the world's best-known and most-published book. Its contents have long since been translated into nearly a thousand different languages and dialects.

Bear with me if you're well acquainted with the Bible and its history. Even if you are, it's worth reminding oneself of just what it is we're talking about.

The word *Bible* comes from the Greek word *biblia*, which simply means "books." The Bible we know is a single book only in the sense that it collects many books between its covers. The Old Testament, of course, is the Bible Jesus knew and used. It consists of thirty-nine separate books. Lamentably, none of the original handwritten manuscripts has survived, the first of which were made about 1,400 years before the birth of Jesus and recopied by hand as the originals deteriorated. Whereas other ancient peoples carved in permanent stone, the Jews wrote on perishable scrolls. Then again, they had a lot to record.

Until 1947, our oldest available copies of the Hebrew Old Testament dated only from the ninth or tenth century *after* Christ. Then Arab shepherds discovered in the caves of Qumran near the Dead Sea copies of the Old Testament that actually antedated Jesus by more than a century. Comparing them with later copies, scholars discovered to their delight that the texts we use today are remarkably faithful to the originals. Not that it was a complete surprise: to ensure accuracy, biblical scribes routinely counted all the words and letters of the originals, matching them to their copies.

The thirty-nine Old Testament books make up three kinds of literature: seventeen histories (Genesis to Esther), five poetical books (Job to Song of Solomon), and seventeen prophetical works. Additional Hebrew holy texts, known collectively as the Apocrypha, were accorded equal respect in the early Greek translation (285–246 B.C.) known as the Septuagint. These writings were included in the original King James Version of the Bible and are still honored as biblical by Roman Catholics.

For ease of study and reference, the Bible is now arranged for us in chapters and verses—a convenience not found in the original books. Stephen Langton, Archbishop of Canterbury (d. 1228), first divided the Bible's books into chapters. More than four centuries later, Robert Stephanus provided the now-familiar verse numbers.

Originally, the Bible was copied onto scrolls of parchment, vellum, or papyrus, some of them as long as forty feet. Late in the first Christian century, an attempt was made to sew individual pages into what we now call a book. A book was not only a more convenient format for reading but more economical as well because copyists could write on both sides of the page.

The lengthy Old Testament was compiled over more than a thousand years as God revealed himself progressively in his creation, then to Noah, Abraham and his family, Moses, David, and generations of Jews. In comparison, the New Testament is relatively brief and was composed in a matter of decades after the death of Jesus. This quick and compact production probably stemmed from the Christian conviction that, in Jesus, God had made his final and complete revelation. The Bible now had a conclusion; after Jesus, there was nothing more to add.

The first generations of Christians expected the world to end during their lifetimes. They could not have conceived of anyone 2,000 years later needing to know Jesus' story. This may account for the random way the books were written and collected. They read more like journalism rather than literature. The Greek in which they are written is simpler than literary Greek.

The New Testament was not imposed on the church; rather, it was chosen by the church as an integral part of its life and worship. The earliest Christians simply read from the Hebrew Bible that Jesus preached from. But by A.D. 200, we know that the church was already making official use of the four Gospels and Paul's letters. The remaining books were more slowly accepted, while many competing books were rejected as fanciful and inconsistent with oral tradition.

Every few years publishers pretend to "discover" a new Gospel they believe unlocks some divine mystery heretofore hidden from us. There is nothing novel about such writings; fanciful accounts were a dime a dozen in the early Christian world and were rejected by the church. It was not until the *fourth century* that the entire church agreed on the contents of the New Testament—forty-two years *after* it had agreed on the Christian creed! Remarkably, it was the same man, St. Athanasius, who crafted the creed and successfully argued for the books that deserved to be included in the New Testament.

Some Christian apologists attempt to defend the accuracy of every detail in the Bible, reckoning that God is in the details. Their efforts are noble and surprisingly successful but ultimately marginal. The Bible's individual books were written at different times for different purposes and different audiences; moreover, the authors' intentions were rarely literal or scientific.

It is tempting to treat the Bible as a portable object of worship that we can wield in the palm of our hand. The president of the United States takes his oath of office with his hand resting on the Scriptures. Christianity is known as a "religion of the book" because it claims the Bible as a fixed reference for its faith. Obviously, that advantage can be overstated.

The Bible comprises Christianity in much the same manner that a cookbook claims to contain all the meals in its recipes. But the words of a recipe cannot feed a hungry person. For that, we need real food to nourish us. George Fox argued that the mere words of the Bible cannot be expected to do what the Spirit does directly—inspire us and motivate us. Quakers are not content with affirming words alone but endeavor to translate them into their lives, turning the printed page into reality.

Jesus lived by the Bible. He did not write it; instead (like Fox after him), he quoted from it, assuring his listeners that he came to fulfill the Scriptures. When challenged by his critics, Jesus typically countered, "But have you not read . . . ?" referring to the Bible as the authority that stood behind what he had to say. His clear message was that his critics had misread or distorted God's revelation. To end an argument, Jesus would proclaim, "It is written . . ." and explain the true meaning of Scripture.

Despite his willingness to simplify the Christian faith, paring it down to its essentials, George Fox was a complete Christian. Late in his life, in a letter to convinced Friends in the Caribbean, he summarized the Quaker faith in a shorthand version of the traditional Christian creed, buttressed by quotations from Scripture. But he made it clear that Scripture and creed were subordinate to the inspiration of the Spirit.

If early biblical accounts appear quaint and fanciful to us, they are nevertheless compelling stories with a clear moral.

Jesus perpetuated the biblical penchant for revealing God's truth through stories. It's clear that his characters—the good shepherd, the good samaritan, the prodigal son, the sower, the owner of the vineyard, and others—are products of the storyteller's art, not real persons. Jesus is not a journalist reporting on individuals with names, addresses, and telephone numbers but a teacher with a gift for creating vivid characters whose stories persuade minds, touch hearts, and change lives.

Some contemporary biblical scholars, not content to merely explain the Bible, attempt to cut away its layers of myth, poetry, and revelation to discover its underlying history—in effect, explaining it away. They are particularly keen to discover the "historical" Jesus, as opposed to the Jesus of faith his eyewitnesses knew.

Pilate and the Pharisees knew the historical Jesus and did not believe his claims, but they took him seriously as a threat and had him executed. Had Pilate written an account of Jesus, it would not be more credible than the Gospels because Pilate failed to take Jesus seriously. Pilate demanded of Jesus, "What is truth?" believing it to be more sophisticated to be skeptical and detached than to believe and act on one's beliefs.

C. S. Lewis noted about Jesus that "he hardly ever gave a straight answer to a straight question." Instead, Jesus preached by proverb, paradox, hyperbole, irony, and parable. As a consequence, it is not easy to believe only what he said. Rather, his followers must assent to *him*. Jesus did not plead, "Listen to what I say." Instead, he commanded, "Follow *me*," and "Learn of *me*." George Fox did that very thing.

The Gospels are, by definition, good news. They are neither biography, history, nor propaganda but testimonials of faith calling for faith. They were never intended to be literal. In approaching the Bible for study, we can't pretend to start from zero-based objectivity. We approach with either belief, curiosity, or skepticism. Even the most doubting person who opens the pages of the Bible today is the unwitting inheritor of a Christian culture, now 2,000 years old, ingrained in the way we all think and in the things we value.

Robert Barclay appropriated the image of a fountain to explain the role of the Bible in Quaker life. Scripture, he said, can be compared to waters that come from a fountain. But it is the Spirit and source of the Inner Light who is the fountain itself.

"IN THE BEGINNING"

Before television and the Internet brought everything instantly into our homes, celebrities were required to move from place to place to address audiences. In the 1950s, when I was growing up, I had the good fortune of meeting some prominent people we could encounter only virtually and electronically nowadays.

I was just sixteen when the great actor Charles Laughton came to our suburban Chicago village to devote an evening to reading to the townspeople. Yes, just to *read*, not play a role.

Sad to say, the custom of reading aloud to one another, like letter writing, is now a lost art in our electronic world of e-mail and cell phones. But my wife and I remain old fashioned enough to read to each other at the end of each day—either something we've written ourselves that day or to share something in print that impressed one of us.

Charles Laughton was vastly more ambitious when he came to visit little La Grange, Illinois, on that Sunday night. He walked onto the bare stage of our high school auditorium balancing a pile of books that reached up to his double chin. Once seated, he removed the top volume and began to read to us from the Bible the familiar account of creation in Genesis. The effect on the audience was like hearing the story for the first time from God himself, telling us how he had come about creating the universe and every living thing.

It is not only a great story but great literature. Genesis is not science or history, however, nor was it intended to be. For example, its account has God accomplishing his work of creation in six "days." Yet God talks about "days" even before he creates the sun and the moon, without which we could not even conceive of days and nights. So the expression "days" is just a dramatic metaphor that is simple to grasp.

While the early Quakers were steeped in Scripture, they were not biblical literalists, betting on every word.

Acknowledging the potential for evil in human nature, Friends agree with the God of Genesis that the world is good and that men and women can purge themselves of evil by living in the Light. Quakers reject the notion of some Christians that God has predestined only a portion of those he has created for salvation. For Friends, the creator is equally the God of *all*, not just a few of his creatures.

Quakers did not fall into the traps that many Christians did as they pondered the meaning of Genesis. Not only did they disregard the notion of Original Sin as a permanent blot on human nature, but they refused to identify the sin of Adam and Eve as being something sexual. Instead, they acknowledged that it was simply the sin of pride and insisted that anyone living in the Light could overcome it without the assistance of baptism, the sacrament of penance, or the intervention of the institutional church.

This helps explain why the early Quakers, even in persecution, were so persistently upbeat. They honored God's own word that the world he made is good.

Friends, of course, are not simply inheritors of the Old Testament but of the New, which gives perspective to the Old. The early Quakers looked back at the story of creation with the help of the Prologue to the Gospel of St. John, which said, "In the beginning was the Word. . . . He was in the beginning with God, and was God. . . . All things were made through him, and without him nothing was made."

This is, of course, an affirmation that the world was made after the pattern of Christ—the "Word" spoken by the creator—in anticipation that God himself would enter his creation as a creature himself, Jesus of Nazareth. The early Quakers would have agreed with Pope Benedict XVI, who stresses that

> for the Christian the Old Testament represents, in its totality, an advance toward Christ; only when it attains him does its real meaning, which was only gradually hinted at, become clear. Thus, every individual part derives its meaning from the whole, and the whole derives its meaning from its end—from Christ.

Quakers are disinclined to look backward, preferring to concentrate on the present—something that is possible because their optimism is rooted in God's faithfulness depicted in the biblical stories and because God is not past but eternally present as the Spirit in the Light.

I mentioned that Genesis departs from the ancient belief that evil was the creation of demonic powers immune from God. In Genesis, by contrast, God overcomes emptiness in order to create what is good. Evil, accordingly, can be blamed not on God or on demons but on our free choice. Evil is a reversion to what existed *before* God created, namely, nothing. There are no creators other than God. Evil is the choice of emptiness over God.

Moving ahead in Genesis, we can see how Quakers made sense of it. When Cain murdered his brother Abel, fearing that he would be murdered in turn, they noted that God protected him—in short, that God was prepared to forgive even the worst of sins.

The story of the Tower of Babel is fanciful but again has a moral. In the story, people seek to storm eternity by their own efforts, building a tower to the skies. God thwarts their efforts by making it impossible for them to communicate with one another. Quakers read the story as simply teaching that God alone saves humankind; people are incapable of saving themselves.

The story of Noah and the ark apparently has some historical basis because there are other ancient accounts of great floods. The moral here for the Quakers was that survival rests on faithfulness and on one's own effort in concert with the grace of God. They also noted that God's other creatures were saved because they did not share man's alienation from the creator.

The destruction of Sodom and Gomorrah has long been cannon fodder for Hollywood because its citizens' sins were assumed to be sexual. The early Quakers merely noted that the story dramatized a reversion to pagan practices by the Canaanites. It also provided a pretext for God to give Canaan to his chosen people, the faithful Israelites.

Although the Old Testament is principally the story of God's dealings with the Israelites, the early Quakers did not consider the book of Genesis to be exclusive. Rather, they noted that "all peoples on earth will be blessed" (Genesis 12:3) through the patriarch Abraham, father of the Jewish nation. It's worth noting that Islam, no less than Judaism and Christianity, fixes on Abraham as the father of their faiths.

Finally, consider the patriarchs—Abraham, Isaac, Jacob, and Joseph (and their wives)—who round out the book of Genesis. Parents today still name their children after these ancient men and women. My wife was named after Isaac's wife—Rebecca.

Anyone reading the patriarchs' stories for the first time is struck by how flawed they were as persons and how primitive the society was that they lived in. They were violent. They were polygamists. They succumbed to fear and envy, and they lied to protect themselves. So in what sense could they be expected to serve as role models for people of faith today?

In just this way: the early Quakers saw in Abraham a man who placed his entire trust in God when he had every reason to doubt the creator and who was tested by God beyond imagination by being ordered to sacrifice the life of his own son. Of course, God stayed Abraham's hand, but looking ahead in the Bible, we will see that God actually sacrifices his own son to death.

In Abraham's case, it is his faith that is the moral of the story. In the commentary to my Bible: "God still looks for the basics—hearts that will, with reckless abandon, risk all to trust in him."

"THE GOOD NEWS"

During the sixteen centuries before the appearance of George Fox, Christians had busied themselves disputing over the details of their common faith, preferring to theologize and speculate rather than simply accept the revelation of Scripture. By the sixteenth century, the lives of Christians were burdened by dogma, tradition, and Church regulations. The Church had effectively superseded Scripture.

During the century prior to the Quaker founder's birth, the great Protestant reformers were not content with simply bringing the reading of the Bible back to the churches and the people. Instead, they continued to argue over indulgences, predestination, good works, grace, the sacraments, and the human and divine natures of Jesus.

It is true that the history of the Christian faith and church is most easily chronicled as the tussle between orthodoxy and heresy. A heresy, so called, is a deviation from traditional faith. Most heresies contain some truth, but they stretch that truth to redefine Christian faith by oversimplifying it.

Orthodoxy, by contrast, holds Christianity to be a rather complex faith full of mysteries that resist explanation. For example, one persistent heresy insisted that to be Christian, one must embrace an impoverished life, whereas orthodoxy set a high value on poverty but insisted that it be freely embraced.

The earliest of the Christian heresies was Gnosticism, which claimed that God's full revelation was restricted to the few rather than to all. Later—and for centuries—Christians disputed over the nature of Jesus. Was he God in a man's body, or was he simply a man especially chosen by God? How could Jesus be both completely human and completely divine? Christians expelled one another from common fellowship on the basis of how they answered this question.

It was George Fox's genius to turn a blind eye to these disputes. Not that Fox dismissed them out of hand; rather, he considered them irrelevant to the average person seeking to lead a godly life. That helps explain why the Quaker movement downplayed or dispensed with so much that other Christians deemed critical to their faith: the Mass, the sacraments, churches, clergy, sermons, and the creed among them.

Here's a homely analogy: if I'm in the market for an affordable and dependable car, I'm likely to dispense with a bunch of options because they cost a great deal extra and add to the number of things that can fail and need fixing. That's choosing simplicity over complexity without losing anything essential. When Fox walked barefoot through Lichfield shouting, "Woe to the people of Lichfield!" he was, in effect, warning them to keep their religion simple.

Looking back over the long centuries of Christian controversy, Fox realized that accretions to the Christian faith had become, at best, distractions from Jesus' message and, at worst, served as weapons to be wielded by one group of Christians against another to no one's advantage.

Fox did not denigrate these aspects of Christian worship or consider them to be valueless. Rather, he said they were unnecessary baggage for anyone to carry who was open to being led by the Light to serve God and others. Fox's choice was to travel light when led by the Light.

Despite his disdain for the professional clergy and preference for silent worship, Fox preached plenty of long sermons himself, and he agreed with the provisions of the written creed. His only argument with churches (or steeple-houses, as he called them) was that they were life-less and costly brick-and-mortar structures, whereas God is free and al-ready present in each individual. Whereas God is portable, a church is not.

Fox's complaint against the clergy was that no class of God's crea-tures is more favored by the creator than any other; *all* are priests and ministers.

Much as he spoke and wrote, Fox did not believe the living faith could be expressed completely in words, be they in sermons or Scrip-ture, but only by following the inner Light, ever open to new leadings. His was a radically stripped-down faith but all the richer for what re-mained.

Of course, Christianity was already an ancient faith by the time Fox appeared on the scene. It was his genius to view it as fresh and alive and to worship a God who is forever young. Had Fox been a student, edu-cated in a seminary, reading Hebrew and Greek, and disputing with the-ologians, he might have been seduced by scholarship and grounded in postbiblical theology rather than perpetually open to the Light of con-tinuing revelation.

Instead, as a young, solitary, and unlettered man tending the flocks and trying to make sense of himself and life, Fox devoured the Bible seeking the answer to his discontent and lack of direction. Eventually, what he discovered was really quite simple, needing no extended analy-sis or theological disputation. In the New Testament, following the brief accounts of Jesus' birth, the Gospels immediately introduce John the Baptist preaching in the desert. John said to everyone who would listen to him, "You must change your hearts and minds—for the kingdom of Heaven has arrived," then proposed a test: "Go and do something to show that your hearts are really changed" (Matthew 3:1–2; 8).

After the Baptist was cast into prison as a troublemaker, Jesus re-peated his cousin's message word for word: "You must change your hearts and minds—for the kingdom of Heaven has arrived" (Matthew 4:17).

This, George Fox realized, was the essence of the Gospel: one must first repent in order to live in the new era dominated by God's Spirit. Unfortunately, itinerant preachers since the Baptist continue to rail on about sin and salvation to a point where many people have become almost immune to the message. Not so George Fox, who accepted wholesale Jesus' prescription that to save one's life, one must first lose it.

We have not the slightest notion what personal shortcomings Fox repented of, but repent he did, and he was immediately opened to the Light, never turning back, enduring imprisonment and persecution not only with grace but with joy. Fox's so-called convincement was neither intellectual nor simply mystical. Rather, it was moral: Fox found the strength to do as the Baptist and Jesus had required—to change not only his mind but his heart and then prove that he was a changed man by what he did from then on.

Here once again is Fox's account of his conversion: "Now I was come up in spirit through the flaming sword into the paradise of God. All things were new and all the creation gave another smell unto me than before, beyond what words can utter. I knew nothing but pureness and innocency and righteousness, being renewed up into the image of God by Christ Jesus, so that I say I was come up into the state of Adam before he fell."

To identify this as simply a "born-again" experience does not do credit to Fox's extraordinary, life-transforming conversion. In America today, close to half of all churchgoing Protestants refer to themselves as "born again," by which they mean they have accepted Jesus as their personal Savior because of an emotional experience rather than by study, example, or argument.

Fox's conversion of heart and mind was clearly emotional, but it was more. Already in his early twenties, he considered himself a derelict, and it was only after all his hopes in men were gone that "I heard a voice which said, 'There is one, even Christ Jesus, that can speak to thy condition,' and when I heard it my heart did leap for joy."

The "condition" in which the young Fox found himself was not irreligion but melancholy, being neither master of himself nor conscious of any vocation or direction in his life. But once convinced that Christ Jesus alone could speak to his condition, Fox began to preach the Gospel. In his first sermon he referred to the passage in Acts in which Paul was literally blinded by light and accepted a commission from Christ to turn the gentiles from darkness to light and from the power of Satan to that of God.

The contemporary Quaker historian John Punshon writes that Fox's message "could easily have been a thing of shreds and patches, stitched up from a variety of other people's religious garments. But it was not. He did not call the Gospel he preached Quakerism but simply 'the Truth.'" And, of course, the early Quakers were known as Friends of the Truth.

What was that Truth? In Fox's own words, he was called to go out in the "briary, thorny wilderness" of the world to proclaim the day of the Lord, to preach repentance, "to turn people from darkness to light that they might receive Christ Jesus."

Fox is usually numbered among the Protestant Reformers. That was never his intention. He never hoped to reform the Church, only the individual. In his words,

> With and by this divine power and spirit of God, and the light of Jesus, I was to bring people off from all their own ways to Christ, the new and living way, and from their churches, which men had made and gathered, to the Church in God, the general assembly written in heaven, which Christ is the head of, and from off the world's teachers made by men to learn of Christ . . . and from off all the world's worships, to know the spirit of Truth in the inward parts. . . . And I was to bring people off from all the world's religions, which are vain. . . . And I was to bring them off from all the world's fellowships, and prayings, and singings, which stood in forms without power. . . . And I was to bring people off from Jewish ceremonies and from heathenish fables and from men's inventions and windy doctrines . . . and all their vain traditions, which they had gotten up since the apostles' days.

Although we lack insight into anything specific that Fox had to repent of, we do know from his own preaching that anyone who would live in the light must choose between self and God. In *Genesis*, it was man's and woman's choice of themselves over God that was the original sin. So Fox surely repented of pride and independence to become utterly dependent on God.

The Quaker founder conceived of two "worlds" existing side by side. One was the world of the Spirit, in which God's will and presence are known to those who repent and are redeemed. That world relies alone on the inward revelation of Christ. Opposed to it was what Fox called "the creature," the world of ordinary unredeemed society, wherein people place their confidence in their own traditions and abilities and in reason and conscience for guidance in matters of faith, enhancing their self-esteem.

So, to live in the Spirit, one cannot rely simply on remorse for one's actual sins, frailties, and misdeeds. Rather, one must exchange self-confidence for total confidence in God. Conversion is a total turning around from self to God. In the words of the hymn "Simple Gifts," it is by "turning, turning, turning, that we turn out right."

In short order, Fox found tens of thousands who accepted the necessity of conversion through repentance. Today, even many Christians are faintly embarrassed that God sent his Son to die on the cross for their sins. Most of us are inclined to think of ourselves as pretty decent persons at heart, not as sinners. We wonder why the human condition required such a drastic remedy. We would all agree to the need for some self-improvement, an occasional moral touch-up—self-applied, of course, whereas George Fox, echoing the Baptist and Jesus, insisted that the Gospel demands a total and permanent makeover.

Still, there are plenty of people today who realize they need redemption because they have hit bottom, so far down in life's dregs that the only way to look is up. Poverty, chronic illness, marital and professional failure, rejection, and addiction bring people down to desperation.

Before I married, I handled a suicide hotline in Chicago from midnight until 6 A.M., on call though the dark hours when hopeful citizens sleep well, while desperate men and women lie awake contemplating putting an end to their misery. During my long, desultory conversations with prospective suicides, their chronic complaint was that they were the victims of life and other people. Only a few phoned to reach out for assistance; most wanted only to share with me their misery and righteous anger at their plight. Unhappily, compassion is insufficient to save people who refuse to take some responsibility for their condition and actively accept a helping hand.

The reason Alcoholics Anonymous (AA) and similar twelve-step programs work is because their members admit they need salvation and cannot accomplish it themselves. The recovering alcoholic does not blame the bottle for his condition; he blames himself but avoids wallowing in guilt. Instead, he reaches beyond himself in hope. For the recovering addict, shame is no longer a deterrent to personal salvation because every AA member acknowledges sharing the same condition. Salvation is the great equalizer. George Fox knew we all need it, that none of us deserve it, and that, to obtain it, we need to repent and accept God's help.

At AA meetings alcoholics confess their sins to fellow sinners: "My name is Adam. I'm an alcoholic, and I confess the foolish things I did when I was drinking. I couldn't keep a job, I lost my wife. My children fear and pity me. I lost my home, my living, and my self-respect. I made a fool of myself. I lost control of my bladder and bowels. I spent the night in jail."

At the end of such a pitiable tale, the speaker unpredictably reveals that he hasn't had a drink in a decade and that he has achieved a new life, with lots of help from others. Nevertheless, he concludes, "I'm still an alcoholic."

Two thousand years ago, when people flocked to John the Baptist at the River Jordan, their motives were strikingly similar to those who attend twelve-step programs today. Repentance and confession are first steps toward the change of heart that prompts us to "do something" to open ourselves to the Light, becoming heirs to hope. Without repentance, we are closed to hope because we refuse to acknowledge our common condition: that we withhold part of ourselves from a loving God. That is the reluctance that George Fox and the early Quakers overcame.

Immediately after Jesus called for a change of heart and mind, he explained how such a person then lives in the Light. It is a radical formula but one that George Fox preached throughout his life:

How happy are those who know their need for God, for the kingdom of Heaven is theirs!

How happy are those who know what sorrow means, for they will be given courage and comfort!

Happy are those who claim nothing, for the whole earth will belong to them!

Happy are those who are hungry and thirsty for true goodness, for they will be fully satisfied!

Happy are the merciful, for they will have mercy shown to them!

Happy are the utterly sincere, for they will see God!

Happy are those who make peace, for they will be known as the sons of God!

Happy are those who have suffered persecution for the cause of goodness, for the kingdom of Heaven is theirs!

And what happiness will be yours when people blame you and ill-treat you and say all kinds of slanderous things against you for my sake! (Matthew 5:3–11)

After his conversion, Fox's own life and mission came to exemplify the Sermon on the Mount.

More than Luther, Calvin, and Knox, George Fox restored primitive Christianity. The other early Reformers aimed to purify the Church and to bring theology more in line with Scripture. They meant to *repair* Christianity. By contrast, Fox chose to return to the simple faith and practice of Jesus' own companions, when there were no priests or sanctuaries but only believers, with their leaders, meeting for worship in their homes—and to a time when the Gospel applied to all peoples, not just the baptized or predestined. He sought to turn back the clock to a time when others marveled at Christ's followers: "How they love one another!"

Fox exemplified the Gospel in other ways, such as his insistence on nonviolence and on sharing with those in need and in his disdain for political interference with religion, rendering to Caesar only the things that are Caesar's but to God all the things that are God's. He exemplified the Gospel also in his conviction that every man and woman is equally cherished by the Creator and deserves to be treated equally—male and female, slave and free, healthy and handicapped, educated and ignorant, rich and poor alike—and in his insistence that one speak the truth and live simply.

We would have to move beyond the Gospels to the Acts of the Apostles in the New Testament to witness dramatic instances of conversion from darkness to light (as in the case of St. Paul) and to Pentecost, when the Spirit literally enlightened the Apostles, giving them the courage to spread the good news of the Gospel.

But already in the Gospels themselves, Friends discern instances of the power of repentance and forgiveness. Typically, when Jesus healed a sick person, he first forgave their sins, rendering them worthy. When Peter repeatedly denied even knowing Jesus, he repented and wept, whereupon Jesus not only forgave him but made him the leader of his first followers.

Fifteen centuries later, once he had repented and was converted, George Fox never looked back. In this, too, he exemplified the earliest Christians, no longer dwelling on sin but on God's promise and on Jesus' command to "be perfect as your heavenly Father is perfect." Today, in a still imperfect and often evil world, we might be inclined to call Fox a cockeyed optimist. In fact, he pursued a life of gratitude for the hope and confidence that he found in the Gospels and in the living Light in which he made his home.

"BLINDED BY THE LIGHT"

By dint of his many published letters, St. Paul is easily the most prominent author of the New Testament. He is also arguably the most reviled of the sacred writers, accused (among other things) of being a misogynist, a scold, a complainer, and, most devastating of all, a fraud—suspected of literally *creating* Christianity as a religion separate from Judaism.

There is a sliver of credibility to that accusation. One can make a case that Paul was the very first Christian. Ironically, the explanation may be that—unlike the other apostles—he was the only one who did not know Jesus of Nazareth during the Lord's sojourn on earth.

At the outset, Jesus' followers (all of them devout Jews) considered themselves to be living an enhancement of Judaism, which they came to call The Way. Their assumption was that one must first of all follow Jewish practices, then Jesus' example in addition.

Paul changed all of that. As Saul, a Pharisaical Jew, he had persecuted Jesus' followers as heretics, only to learn the folly of his ways when he was remarkably converted by being blinded and thrown from his horse and hearing the voice of Jesus. The critical lesson in Paul's conversion was that Jesus and his Kingdom belonged to all the people of the world without exception. Paul effectively severed the connection between Jewish birth and practice—and life in Christ's Spirit.

The earliest generations of Quakers—all of them devout Christians—learned from St. Paul that all of the world's peoples are God's peoples and that there are no distinctions among them. Man and woman, slave and free, rich and poor, ignorant and educated, dark skinned and light, healthy or sick—all were equally cherished by God and given the same responsibilities and hope. Nor did differences in language and culture matter. As the early Friends would express it, the Spirit of Christ resided in absolutely *everyone* without exception.

Those original apostles who devoted the remainder of their lives to converting their fellow Jews to Christ failed. Moreover, they only reluctantly endorsed Paul's mission to extend the new faith to the world's people without burdening them with the necessity of circumcision and dietary laws.

By contrast, Paul traveled constantly and extensively around the known world, principally to the lands surrounding the Mediterranean basin. He was a Roman citizen, which gave him freedom of movement and some protection from authorities. Typically, he introduced himself to a new city at its synagogue. There were pockets of Jews in all the major cities of the empire. From there he branched out, preaching a Gospel of freedom, hope, and immortality to everyone.

He was imprisoned for his efforts, just as George Fox would be sixteen centuries later for preaching the identical message. It's arguable that Paul and Fox were imprisoned precisely because they were successful.

I'm inclined to believe that Paul's only obvious shortcoming is that he wasn't Jesus, nor did he pretend to be anything like the Lord he served. He was a motivator, an explainer, an organizer, and a total disciple. Unlike the original apostles, he was celebrated not for working wonders but simply for being effective.

It's a stretch, of course, but I am tempted to compare Jesus and his apostle Paul as Latter-Day Saints today might compare their founder, Joseph Smith, and his lieutenant, Brigham Young. Smith was the founder and inspiration of the Mormons. Young, Smith's disciple, never competed with the founder. Instead, after Smith's death, Young turned inspiration into an effective religious movement and institutionalized it worldwide.

In the seventeenth century, George Fox found himself in a similar position as that of Paul in the first. England had an official religious faith, Anglicanism, and any dissident was pegged as a Nonconformist. Fox attempted to preach in his nation's established churches but was summarily ejected. Nor was he notably successful in converting rank-and-file members of the Church of England.

But he did gain a hearing from the ranks of other nonconformists, who found both structure and inspiration in his fledgling Religious Society of Friends of the Truth and were responsible for the rapid early growth of the movement.

Like St. Paul, Fox became a latter-day apostle to the Gentiles, encouraging the emigration of Friends to the New World and personally carrying the Gospel of the Inner Light to Europe, the Caribbean, and to mainline America. Just as Christianity did not prevail against Judaism in

Israel, Fox's Gospel of the Inner Light could not defeat the Church of England in the mother country. So it took on the world.

It was wildly successful in the English colonies of the New World, where even Anglicans were bristling at the micromanaging of their churches in America by authorities back in England.

Fox's Society of Friends of the Truth was successful in the New World not only because of its buoyant spirit, confidence in human nature, and radical democracy but also because its simplicity suited the relatively primitive society of the American colonies.

Whereas the established churches sought to reproduce their brick-and-mortar houses of worship after the European model, the Quakers merely gathered where and when they could—as the early Christians had—and sought inspiration and simplicity together. Unburdened of an ordained ministry and church hierarchy, they became autonomous.

During his lifetime, George Fox left some 400 epistles, written during the forty-seven years between 1643 and 1690. They began with pastoral letters to small groups of Friends in the north of England, then expanded to include epistles to Jamaica, New England, Barbados, Virginia, Germany, Holland, the Palatinate, Danzig, Sweden, and Switzerland. He also wrote to individual Friends in the traveling ministry, to women's meetings, and to "Friends that have black and Indian slaves."

Like St. Paul, Fox's emphasis is on exhorting the faithful to unity, love, tenderness with the weak, and with purity and faithfulness to the Truth as revealed in Jesus Christ. Also like St. Paul, he was keen to extinguish dissension and ambition within local meetings of Friends.

In his letters, Paul claimed authority as "a servant of Christ Jesus, called to be an apostle and set apart for the gospel of God" (Romans 1:1). Fox, typically, was more verbose in justifying his ministry:

> First, I was sent out by the Lord God, in his eternal light and power, to preach the word of life . . . and to turn people to the light . . . that all might be reconciled to God, by the word; and that all might believe in the light, which is the life in Christ the Word; and so become children of the light, and to know Christ . . . and their faith to stand in him, who is the author and finisher of it; and to turn people to the spirit, which they had quenched, vexed and grieved, and rebelled against; that in the holy spirit they might see before the spirit of error was . . . that in the spirit they may know God and Christ, and the scriptures, which were given forth from it; and in the same spirit,

they might all have fellowship one with another, and with the Father
and Son . . . so to preach the everlasting gospel, power of God . . .
that brings life and immortality to light, in all that do receive it . . .
which gospel I received not of man, nor by man, but of the Lord Jesus Christ, by his holy spirit sent down from heaven. (Epistle 317)

Although it is not obvious, Fox used eighteen references to the
New Testament to justify his commission to preach the Gospel. One
third of the references come directly from Paul's own epistles.

Nevertheless, while he relied on Scripture, Fox was careful to distinguish between mere biblical words and the Word that is Christ. Here
he echoed Paul, who acknowledged of his revelation that "I put this in
human terms . . ." (Romans 6:19). Fox adds,

In the beginning was the Word; though since the beginning were the
words and letters, for the scriptures of truth are the word of God,
and the words of Christ. . . . So the Word was in the beginning, and
Christ's name is called the Word of God; but Christ is neither called
scriptures nor writings. (Epistle 249)

Fox appropriated additional themes from Paul's epistles in his own
letters sixteen centuries later. They resonate with all Quakers today:

"All things work together for good to them that love God" (Ro-
mans 8:28).
"Let love be without dissimulation" (Romans 12:9).
"If it be possible, as much as it lieth in you, live peaceably with all
men" (Romans 12:18).
"Be not overcome of evil, but overcome evil with good" (Romans
12:21).
"Let us therefore follow after the things that make for peace" (Romans 14:19).
"For the temple of God is holy, which temple ye are" (1 Corinthians 3:17).
"And now abideth faith, hope, charity, these three; but the greatest
of these is charity" (1 Corinthians 13:13).
"Not of the letter, but of the spirit; for the letter killeth, but the
spirit giveth life" (1 Corinthians 16:22).
"Seeing then that we have such hope, we use great plainness of
speech" (2 Corinthians 3:12).

It was to St. Paul that Martin Luther referred when he laid the foundations of the Protestant Reformation. Personally convinced of his own sinful nature and persuaded that every human is born under condemnation, Luther rejected the prevailing notion that one could earn one's salvation through good works and fixed instead on God's promise that one could be saved through faith.

More than a century later, Fox objected to the joint Catholic–Protestant premise that humankind is born into sin. He acknowledged the dark side of human nature and the prevalence of evil, but he believed that by living in the light of Christ, one might actually approach perfection.

Fox rejected the notion that one could gain God's favor through ritual or good deeds, but neither could one merit salvation by simply *believing* in Christ. Rather, Fox preached, one must live in Christ's spirit in order to partake of the covenant.

When St. Paul speaks of "justification by faith" (Romans 1:17), the apostle's sense is similar to a "not guilty" judgment in a court of law. To be sure, in rendering a verdict of "not guilty," judge and jury are not proclaiming someone's innocence—only that the person will not be held to account for the offense.

Fox agreed that one's sins are forgiven by dint of faith and that the follower of Christ is bound to do good by his faithfulness. But Fox did not obsess over guilt and innocence. Rather, he recognized that God through Christ had liberated the world and renewed the old covenant with humankind. By living in Christ and entering into the new covenant with fellow Christians, one need no longer fret about sin and salvation. Whether Jew or Gentile, all who believe in Jesus' good news and enter into it are members of the family of Abraham, the father of nations, with their sins being forgiven.

But no one is saved by simply believing in justification by faith in the form of an insurance policy that one files away in a safe deposit box. One must live by faith. And here Fox and the early Quakers learned from Paul's personal example—to be wise fools, strong weaklings, failures in purely human terms; to be persecuted and imprisoned; and to keep the faith not by mere acquiescence to revelation but by living in the Spirit and proclaiming the Gospel to the world.

As Paul put it, the kingdom of God is not a matter of talk but of power. And Fox and his followers were confident of speaking truth to power, confident that no power could resist the truth.

Just as Paul liberated Judaism from its legalism, George Fox liberated Christianity from its formality, from its institutionalism, and from church politics. Christ had freed man and woman from themselves to live the Gospel, which is to say to live every present moment in God's Spirit with the sure hope of eternal life in God's company. Like Adam before his Fall, the faithful could now walk once again with their God in the Garden.

· 6 ·

The Good Quaker

When true simplicity is gained,
To bow and to bend we shan't be ashamed,
To turn, turn, will be our delight,
Till by turning, turning, we turn out right.

—"Simple Gifts"

$\mathcal{A}$s a fledgling Friend, I asked the clerk of our meeting what was "normative" in Quaker belief and practice. I was really asking, "What, minimally, makes for a *good* Quaker?" His unhesitating reply has echoed in my mind ever since. "By their fruits you shall know them," he said, quoting Jesus.

Friends look first of all to how people actually behave—not to the creeds they profess or to how well they express themselves. Accordingly, it is well nigh impossible to be a Quaker and to be a hypocrite. Friends don't dress up for Sunday worship, so we see one another as everyone else does during the rest of the week. In worship, we maintain silence, so we can't impress one another with our education, our knowledge, or our facility with words.

One of the first things I remarked about Friends is that they don't talk a lot about themselves. In Washington, D.C., where my wife and I pursued our careers, the first question to be asked of a stranger at a social event is, "What do you do?" Meaning, "What do you do for a living?" My fellow Quakers, nearly all of whom pursue professional lives in Washington, never identify themselves with their careers or their status. After all these years I still haven't a clue what many of my fellow Friends do in the workaday world, let alone how educated or well off they are or how much they contribute financially to the meeting.

Over time, however, what becomes obvious is whether an individual is personally generous, reliable, and patient. That's because, lacking the benefit of clergy and staff, every member is equally responsible for the meeting's needs. For example, I am, among other things, our meeting's window washer, and my wife is responsible for buying food and supplies in bulk. Granted, these do not make us sterling Quakers, but they help make it possible for all of us to form and sustain a community of worship and service not unlike that of the earliest Christians.

Over time, there are other, more subtle revelations. We have acquired an appreciation of the devotion that binds our married Friends to their spouses and their children. And we sense the loneliness and trials of some of our single, divorced, and elderly members as well as those whose spouses choose not to join them in worship. Worshipping in common silence, we somehow feel our comradeship as we hold one another "in the Light." Because a Quaker meeting offers no premium for one's status, ambition, or worldly success, it is utterly egalitarian.

So what is it makes for a "good" Quaker? Surely not the content or sophistication of his or her faith because many Friends freely admit to their uncertainties. Nor to one's righteousness because Friends do not equate religion with mere rule keeping. Nor even to accepting Jesus as one's personal Savior, although many of us do. To require that would be to deny that there is that of God in *everyone*, not just Christians, but in skeptics, sinners, and those raised as Muslims, Jews, or Buddhists.

Nor does goodness require a Friend to be "born again" or to be baptized by water because the emotional experience of spiritual rebirth has eluded many of us and because Quakers believe the traditional sacraments, while worthy, are not essential to a godly life, if only because the majority of God's people around the world don't have access to them as Christians do.

Although Quakers speak little, they do sing, putting their own stamp on the eighteenth-century Shaker hymn "Simple Gifts," professing their belief that "by turning, turning," they will turn out right. "Turning," of course, is another word for conversion, which Friends believe is a lifelong endeavor. Jesus and his cousin, John the Baptist, both proclaimed God's kingdom with these words: "You must change your hearts and minds . . ." (Matthew 3:2). So Quakers do not aspire merely to be on their best behavior but to be of good heart and mind—a much more demanding conversion.

Friends in any case do not pursue virtue for righteousness' sake but because it makes for peace with God, with oneself, and with one's neighbor. They embrace simplicity of life not as piety or sacrifice but as a practical path, acknowledging that one's appreciation for life's simple gifts grows in direct proportion as one's further ambitions and demands are curbed. Life satisfaction eludes those who demand more than the necessities and simple comforts they already possess in abundance.

Quakers shrink from being considered virtuous, preferring simply to follow their consciences, consistent with being generous, responsible, and reliable. More than most other believers, Friends associate reliability with telling the truth. Wary of flattery, they hold that honesty—even when it occasionally offends—is preferable to evasion.

The nation's courts have long since accommodated Quaker resistance to confining truth telling to testimony given under oath. Today, all witnesses are required only to *affirm* or *promise* that they are telling the truth, the whole truth, and nothing but the truth.

To be sure, a Quaker conscience can often be a formidable thing, propelling many Friends into public advocacy, notably against war, poverty, the death penalty, cruelty to animals, and in favor of environmental protection and equal rights and opportunity. Beyond these concerns, some Friends are also virulently pro-choice and strenuous advocates for vegetarianism, gay marriage, and alternative medicine. But many other Friends take opposing views. While the Quaker conscience does not demand its members be pacifists, their vehicles more often sport bumper stickers claiming "War is not the answer" than "Honk if you love Jesus."

The powerful Quaker conscience is institutionalized in the work of two national organizations, the Friends Committee on National Legislation (FCNL), a public policy organization on Capitol Hill, and the American Friends Service Committee (AFSC), an international aid organization headquartered in Philadelphia. With its British counterpart, AFSC was honored with the Nobel Peace Prize for its work in European reconstruction following World War II. Neither FCNL's nor AFSC's agenda perfectly reflects the consciences of individual Friends, but they tend to mirror a Quaker consensus on values that deserve to be protected in American public life. More about them later.

To better grasp the character of contemporary Quakers, it is worth examining what, by comparison, constitutes a "good" Jew, Muslim,

Catholic, and Protestant according to members of those faiths. In each instance, goodness requires being "observant," that is, showing up and joining in prayer and worship and honoring religious discipline. For the good Muslim, that means prayer five times each day; for the Catholic, it is attendance at Mass every Sunday and holy day and frequenting the sacraments; and for many evangelical Protestants, it means agreeing to be regularly tithed a portion of one's income.

To be a good Jew, one must not only adhere to ritual and dietary requirements but also follow strictly 613 commandments—including 248 obligations and 365 prohibitions.

In every case, whichever faith one professes, "goodness" reflects adherence to rules, and a pious life is defined as a disciplined one.

Still, the faithful rule keeper may not necessarily lead a loving, generous, or self-sacrificing life. Quakers, by contrast with other religious traditions, dispense as far as possible with rules, except as they are practical and make for community and concord. Instead, Friends seek the law's spirit rather than merely compliance with its letter.

"By their fruits you shall know them" requires not just compliance but service, generosity, love, and self-sacrifice—practical virtues that are well nigh impossible to express in the form of rules. In this sense, goodness (within all faith traditions) is not a passive virtue but an active one. Goodness requires one to *do* good for others.

The permanent availability of forgiveness is among the most attractive qualities of Christianity, allowing the sinner to pick himself up, dust himself off, and start all over again. But forgiveness assumes the sinner is sincerely repentant, resolves to be faithful, and makes love the overwhelming rule of his life.

Observant Jews and Muslims sense that many Christians overindulge God's willingness to forgive them their serial sins and are too quick to forgive themselves because they are motivated by good intentions. Despite Americans' overwhelming religiosity, Muslim fundamentalists fault our society as hypocritically permissive, sensual, undisciplined, sentimental, and worldly. They have a point.

By simple living, truth telling, and mutual service, Quakers seek to avoid the moral traps to which human nature is prone. Preferring silence to outspoken piety, they let their lives speak for their beliefs.

Quaker historian John Punshon first encountered the Quakers when he was an undergraduate at Oxford. Raised as a Baptist, he was curious about people who worshipped in silence but was unprepared for sitting for an hour of a Sunday with a group of strangers who had nothing to say for themselves or about God.

He fidgeted but persisted as seekers do to this day who respond to the quiet welcome of a local Quaker meeting. The Oxford Friends made no fuss over Punshon, and it was only over time that he came to appreciate that Quakers leave it to God's initiative to lead people to them. After a time, he was able to discern when a meeting was successful, even when not a word of testimony was offered, because he sensed that there was a single silence that everyone entered, incorporating every person's openness to God's initiative.

What happens in a Quaker meeting? It is impossible to say for sure because the silence is left behind and no one reports on what, if anything, they have taken away from it. On occasion, individuals feel moved to break the silence to share a thought, a story, a concern, or an inspiration. Sometimes, the message is helpful; occasionally, it is simply an intrusion and a distraction.

For example, my wife recently stood up in meeting to share something she had learned from the obituary of the late Simon Wiesenthal, the death camp survivor who devoted the remainder of his life to exposing Nazi war criminals. As the Allies advanced near war's end, a German officer fleeing the camp had asked him, "After the war, what will you tell your liberators about us?" The prisoner replied, "I will tell them the truth." Whereupon the officer laughed: "They will never believe you." From that moment, Wiesenthal vowed to dedicate his life to telling the truth.

Becky's story was meant to underscore the power of truth telling. Instead, her testimony prompted other Friends to tell stories about how hard it is for them to face the truth about themselves and others. One teacher actually wept as she recounted her tale of being abused by a violent student.

Some of the best testimony I have heard in Quaker meetings echo a lesson taught me by a wise editor who advised me to refrain from preaching to people, reminding them instead of truths they already accept but seldom take time to ponder or put in practice.

"Friendly persuasion," in short, is not argumentative. It seeks not to score points but to win hearts. People are persuaded only when it is in their ultimate interest to change their hearts and minds and to put their beliefs into practice. The goodness of individual Quakers is measured not by the beliefs they hold but by their willingness to act on their faith, even in the face of opposition and even persecution.

Most Quakers avoid moral self-assessment. In this respect, their model is Jesus, who challenged his flatterers: "Why do you call me good? No one is good—except God alone" (Luke 18:19).

Quaker children attend Sunday School while their parents are worshipping together, then join the adults for the final ten minutes of the roughly hour-long silence. As you might imagine, the absence of noise or speech is foreign to the youngest of the boys and girls, so joining a roomful of silent strangers can spook them. I suspect that most of the youngsters have no experience of their parents being absolutely quiet for so long a period at home.

I was once asked by a Sunday school teacher to help the young Quakers understand what the adults were up to. Here is a potion of what I told them:

"Friends believe that vocal prayers, singing, and sermons can be distractions from worship, which is communicating with God in our hearts and minds—something that requires silence.

"Of course, you or I could sit alone in silence at home or anywhere else, but Jesus advised that 'wherever two or three are gathered together in my name, I am there with you.' We worship together because we are responsible for one another.

"Every athlete knows that he or she must learn the correct moves from the start. That doesn't guarantee that they will become top performers, but by starting with the right technique they can only improve. The worst thing athletes can do is learn the wrong moves because then they must first *un*learn what they are doing wrong before they can improve.

"Unlike athletics, when you worship in silence, no one is awarding you a score. There are no tests. But if you start wrong, you will be bored and discouraged, the hour will seem endless, and you will accomplish little or nothing.

"So do some thinking or reading before you come to the meeting. Recall what happened in the past week that is worth your thinking about and understanding better. Maybe it's something that happened at home or in school. In any case, bring an experience to ponder and to share with God.

"Close your eyes to escape distractions. Then relax. Nothing is going to happen for a whole hour, so settle down. Start a silent conversation with God, looking back over the past week. Today you're a week older. Ask yourself: Am I a week wiser?

"If there are things you are sorry for, now is the time to admit them and ask God's forgiveness. If there are things to be thankful for, say you're grateful. If there are some things you need for yourself (not just things you *want*), say so.

"Then ask God to care for the needs of your friends and others. Ponder how you might actually be able to help them yourself.

"During all of this you will be distracted. Don't *fight* distractions. That makes them too important. Just ignore them. Get back to the subject.

"Perhaps half an hour has passed during which you've done all the talking. God already knew what you were going to say anyway, so you've really been talking to yourself—still, it's good to get in touch with yourself.

"Now it's time to start listening. Let God speak to you. He won't use words, but he'll introduce thoughts into your head and feelings in your heart. At the end of worship you may leave having decided to act or feel or think differently than you have up until now. Rest assured, you will be a slightly different and better person for having opened yourself to God.

"There's an old clock in our meetinghouse. We use it to mark time, but of course the clock itself has no sense of time passing—it just ticks away. Let the clock lull you from the sense of time passing. If you ask them, your parents will admit that the passage of time makes them regret the past and feel anxious about the future. So, during worship, pretend that there is no past or future, but just the present moment. Let God fill that moment.

"St. Paul says that once you get the hang of worship, you will discover that you are no longer the one doing the praying—rather, it is God's Spirit in you. Think about it. That means that God is praying to God in you. You're just paying attention to what's going on.

"Occasionally, someone will stand up in the meeting and speak about something that has inspired him or her. Sometimes you will find the messages helpful, at other times just distractions. But be respectful: these are things on people's minds that they labor over.

"Finally, spend the last few minutes meditating—not thinking *about* anything, but just emptying your mind so God can fill it. Let God do the heavy lifting when you worship. That's inspiration."

People who know next to nothing about Quakers are aware that Friends are dedicated to peace. There are always Friends on the barricades, peacefully protesting violence and war. Their preoccupation with peace probably stems from the extreme violence their forebears suffered. During war and during the peacetime draft, many young Quaker men became conscientious objectors. Their motivation was not cowardice but a conviction that life is precious and that violence cannot be disarmed by further violence.

Over the centuries, Quakers have gone to extraordinary lengths to sow peace. Just before World War II, they sent a delegation to Nazi Germany to attempt to persuade Adolf Hitler to choose peace rather than war. In the seventeenth century, the Quaker Mary Fisher traveled to Constantinople to plead with the sultan to stop persecuting Jews and Christians in his territories.

As I noted at the outset, Tom Fox, a Quaker peacemaker formerly of our meeting, was on a mission of reconciliation in Iraq in 2006 when he was abducted by terrorists and killed. It will take decades or longer to judge whether his mission was an utter failure or a partial success.

If, in retrospect, peacemaking seems foredoomed, recall that St. Francis of Assisi centuries ago attempted to persuade the Saracens to end the Crusades. That beloved saint failed, yet the very effort of sowing peace provides a counterweight to those who resort to war for insufficient provocation. Even General William Tecumseh Sherman, who devastated the American South to end the Civil War, acknowledged that the only legitimate purpose of war is to secure the peace.

Today, Quaker relief services take it upon themselves to do more than provide immediate assistance to victims of war and natural tragedy. They remain on-site, often for years, to restore peace to countries and communities traumatized by violence.

If you believe, as Friends do, that there is that of God in everyone, then you, too, are serving God when you serve them.

· 7 ·

The Holy Experiment

Let us do our duty, and leave the rest to God.

—William Penn

*W*hen Quakers departed England to settle in the New World, George Fox bade them farewell with this caution:

> Friends . . . going over to plant and make outward plantations in America, keep your own plantations in your hearts, with the spirit and power of God, that your own vines and lilies be not hurt.

Fox's counsel was that Friends attend to the Inner Light rather than the ways of the world. Unfortunately, the settlers were required to assume the responsibilities of civil government.

Just as the Puritans intended Massachusetts to be God's City on a Hill, Friends regarded Pennsylvania as a Holy Experiment in approximating heaven on earth. Ironically, to ensure the godliness of the colony, they were required to dominate its politics.

To be sure, Friends were not reluctant politicians, but their religious faith got in the way of their effectiveness. After only a century, they abdicated public office altogether. Thomas Jefferson spoke critically of them as

> a religious sect . . . acting with one mind, and that directed by the mother society in England. Dispersed, as the Jews, they still form, as those do, one nation, foreign to the land they live in. They are Protestant Jesuits, implicitly devoted to the will of their superior, and forgetting all duties to their country in the execution of the policy of their order.

It was a harsh judgment on a people who were as democratically disposed, fair-minded, and religiously tolerant as Jefferson himself and even more egalitarian.

In colonial America, Pennsylvania was as dominated by Fox's disciples as Utah would be by the followers of Joseph Smith and Brigham Young in later centuries. The first Friend to arrive in America (1655 or 1656) was the missionary Elizabeth Harris, who traveled around the Chesapeake. By 1657, less than a decade after its founding in England, Fox's faith grew to exert a significant influence in at least ten American colonies, helping to define the national character and the expectations of all Americans.

Persecuted in Puritan Massachusetts and Anglican Virginia, Quakers influenced religious and political life elsewhere in the colonies. For thirty-six terms, Rhode Island was led by Quaker governors. By 1700, half the population of Newport was Quaker. Until 1701, Friends constituted the only organized religious denomination in North Carolina. In addition to controlling Pennsylvania by royal charter, they governed West Jersey and East Jersey until they were combined into the single royal colony of New Jersey.

With the waning of Puritan orthodoxy, large Quaker populations settled in southern and western Massachusetts. By sheer force of numbers, they were influential in the social and political life of Maine, New Hampshire, New York City, Long Island, and towns around Boston. Moreover, by 1780, there were 3,000 Friends in Maryland and 5,000 in Virginia. In the middle of the eighteenth century, the Quaker population in America exceeded that in Great Britain.

In 1681, in settlement of a debt owed by King Charles II to his father, William Penn received a charter for the colony that came to bear his family name. Persuaded that his charter came not from a king but from divine providence, Penn determined to establish a model Christian community as a "Holy Experiment." He established a democratically elected assembly and ensured freedom of conscience and the right to worship according to one's own convictions. He discouraged bureaucracy and abolished tithes.

Pennsylvania's prisons became workhouses for the rehabilitation of criminals. All children to the age of twelve were taught a useful trade or skill. As far as possible consistent with the laws of the mother country, Penn also severely restricted slavery and the death penalty in the colony.

The Holy Experiment clearly succeeded in this: it proved that religious tolerance was not inimical to political stability.

Quaker character stood in sharp contrast to that of the Puritans. Where the Pilgrims were exclusive, dogmatic, hierarchical, righteous, and quick to persecute dissent, Friends were democratic, informal, mystical, tolerant, and nonviolent. Fearless missionaries, they openly sought persecution as validation of their faith.

Friends believed that all persons of both sexes and all races and nationalities were equal in God's sight and deserved to be treated equally. Quakers were neighborly with native Americans, purchasing rather than stealing land from them, and finding a kinship between tribal beliefs and their own.

Back in Great Britain, of course, Quakers were excluded from politics and the professions because they were Nonconformists. By contrast, in the New World—especially in Pennsylvania—they were actually required to govern. Unfortunately, certain articles of the Quaker faith, applied too literally, impeded their ability to provide security for those fellow citizens who did not share their religious convictions.

With the Puritans, Quakers shared a hatred of tyranny, plus a moral earnestness reminiscent of the Old Testament prophets, pitting the life of the spirit against that of the world.

With growing affluence, the Puritans softened their dogmatism and made compromises with wealth and comfort. American Quakers, by contrast, embraced simplicity and plain living with an almost obsessive tenacity. Unlike the Puritans, Friends were religiously tolerant, but like them, they were anything but indifferent about their convictions, which they held tenaciously, ultimately to the detriment of their ability to rule a multiethnic and cultural Pennsylvania.

Whereas the Puritans had sought to build their ideal City on a Hill by adherence to Old Testament strictures, Friends were persuaded that they could establish the kingdom of God on earth by personal obedience to inward Divine revelation. They felt they had grasped a Principle (always spelled with a capital P) that could revolutionize life on earth. That Principle was the presence of a Divine Light in every person, no matter how sophisticated or uneducated, that directly reveals God's will to him or her and calls for adherence to that will.

The modern Quaker philosopher Rufus Jones acknowledged that the colonial Quakers risked everything they had on the truth of this

Principle. They were persuaded that by obedience to the prompting of the Holy Spirit, they could create the Peaceable Kingdom in their time and place, where the lamb would lie with the lion unmolested.

In short order, by dint of thrift, fair dealing, and hard work, Friends made early Pennsylvania the most prosperous and peaceful of the colonies. "From a wilderness," the Quaker Richard Townsend noted in 1727, "the Lord, by his good hand of Providence, hath made it a fruitful field." But before long, as former Librarian of Congress Daniel Boorstin observes, "the Quakers realized that their religious doctrines, if construed strictly, would put difficulties in the way of their running a government. It was one thing to live by Quaker principles, quite another to rule by them."

Boorstin argues that the American Quakers crippled their political and evangelical effectiveness "not by being false to their teachings, but by being too true to them." In the tradition of the Gospel, the great Quaker prophets had opted for the spirit of the law over its letter, but succeeding generations of followers increasingly preferred the strict letter as proof of their faithfulness.

The Quaker faith disdains dogma and rejects creeds as wordy formulas that obscure God's direct and personal revelation to each individual. Nevertheless, some beliefs common among Friends compromised their ability to govern. For example, Fox himself took literally Jesus' prohibition of oath taking.

As it turned out, Great Britain accommodated individual Quakers by allowing them to substitute a mere "affirmation" for an oath. But in Pennsylvania, Quaker officials refused not only to take oaths but also to *administer* oaths to non-Quakers in their jurisdictions—making it impossible for them to act as witnesses in trials of persons accused of crimes. Their position hardened to the point where they persuaded themselves that oaths were not only unnecessary to ensure honesty in courts of law but also evil in themselves.

Moreover, as Quaker pacifism hardened into political principle, it became increasingly difficult to ensure the peace and protect the populace from Native American, French, Spanish, and domestic violence within their borders. While acknowledging that the fundamental duty of any government was to protect the people, the Quaker majority in the Pennsylvania assembly could not bring themselves to compromise their peace testimony to actually ensure tranquility even by the defensive use of arms.

When the Puritans in Great Britain overthrew the monarchy and proclaimed a commonwealth under Oliver Cromwell, William Penn fell out of favor in the mother country and went into hiding. After the restoration of the Stuarts under Charles II, Pennsylvania came under royal governance for two years (1692–1694), primarily because the colonial Quakers refused to cooperate in Pennsylvania's defense.

Once self-rule was restored, Penn generously reduced his executive power as governor in favor of his Quaker-dominated assembly. But he found its members ungrateful. Meanwhile Penn's eldest son renounced his father's faith, and Penn's steward was discovered to have defrauded the great man of the bulk of his wealth.

Discouraged, Penn sought to sell the Holy Experiment altogether. But when ten years later, on the verge of a sale, Penn suffered a crippling stroke, the transaction fell through, and the great man lingered as an invalid until he died six years later. During that time Pennsylvania was held in trusteeship because of Penn's debts. On his death it passed to his second wife, Hannah.

"Let us do our duty, and leave the rest to God," Penn had counseled his fellow Pennsylvanians in 1701. But it became increasingly problematic for the Quakers to govern dutifully and still pursue the purity of their faith.

Although English Quakers had no role in colonial government, the London Yearly Meeting constantly intervened to shape Quaker policy in Pennsylvania, sending emissaries to press the American Friends to accept rigid orthodoxy. There was to be no compromise on taking or administering oaths or on pacifism and capital punishment.

Daniel Boorstin laments that "whenever tested, the Quakers chose the solution which kept themselves pure, even though others might have to pay the price." As to pacifism, the Pennsylvania Friends attempted for a century to evade the issue by ensuring that their deputy governor be a congenial non-Quaker. In effect, it was the second in command who provided for the colony's common defense, leaving the pacifist consciences of the governor and Quaker-dominated assembly untainted.

When, in April 1689, England declared war against the French and demanded the Quakers defend their colony and establish a militia, a member of Penn's council scoffed, saying there was no danger to Pennsylvanians except from "the bears and wolves." A dozen years later, when England was fighting *both* France and Spain, war was duly declared in Pennsylvania, but the Quaker assembly politely excused itself from raising any funds for defense, pleading,

Were it not that the raising money to hire men to fight or kill one another is matter of Conscience to us and against our Religious Principles, we should not be wanting, according to our small abilities, to Contribute to those designs.

When a new war began in 1739, Spanish privateers sailed on the Delaware threatening the colony. Rather than raise a militia in Pennsylvania's defense or provision a British garrison, the Quakers in the assembly chose to paralyze the government by preventing any legislation. For a time in 1741, they even withheld their governor's salary. When, in 1745, the governor finally wrested an appropriation to provision English troops, he was careful to mention only food, not arms.

From the outset, the Quakers had treated the Indians fairly and generously, seeking to cultivate their friendship. But the Indians were not altogether pacific. Rather, they warred tribe against tribe and harassed isolated settlers. Some took sides against the English colonists during the French and Indian War. Despite massacres in western Pennsylvania, the Quaker-dominated assembly chose to make a large cash gift to the Indians in 1748, at the same time that they refused to provide for the defense of Philadelphia. The well-intentioned bribes were ineffective. When the colony forged an alliance in 1742 with the Iroquois, the Delawares within Pennsylvania's borders considered it a provocation.

By 1745, a strong compromise party emerged in the assembly, led by Benjamin Franklin. It was neither pro- nor anti-Quaker, only insisting on the duty of the colonial government to protect its citizenry. If the Quaker legislators could not do so on principle, Franklin's party argued, then they should allow others to rule and defend Pennsylvania. Franklin himself managed to raise private funds to form and equip a militia of 10,000 men, but even it proved inadequate. A decade later Franklin was still lamenting that "our frontier people [are] continually butchered," and concluded, "I do not believe we shall ever have a firm peace with the Indians, till we have well drubbed them."

Franklin's popular party proposed making all male colonists subject to military service, commutable by payment of a fine. Militia officers would be democratically elected. According to the proposal, Quakers would not have to bear arms themselves but would have to help pay for the colony's defense.

By 1756, although they made up fewer than one-fourth of all Pennsylvanians, Quakers still held more than three-fourths of the seats in the colonial assembly. They ignored Franklin's appeal.

Meanwhile in London, the English government, concerned for the protection of the colonists, considered permanently disqualifying any Quaker from holding public office in Pennsylvania. Dr. John Fothergill, a respected elder of London Yearly Meeting, spelled out the governor's case against the Quaker assemblymen to American Friends:

> . . . you are unfit for government. You accept our publick trust, which at the same time you acknowledge you cannot discharge. You owe the people protection, & yet withhold them from protecting themselves. Will not all the blood that is spilt lye at your doors? and can we . . . sit still and see the province in danger of being given up to a merciless enemy without endeavoring its rescue?

London Quakers negotiated a compromise with the English government, permitting members of the Pennsylvania assembly to resign from office voluntarily. In the late spring of 1756, the governor and his council declared war on the Shawnee and Delaware Indians, which forced the issue. Quaker members abdicated rather than support their colony's armed defense, and the colony passed permanently into governance by non-Quakers.

In this respect, Penn's Holy Experiment came to an end, although many Quaker politicians believed they could regain office once immediate hostilities ended. But when the American Revolution began some twenty years later, Quakers were once again compromised. Although they refused to pay taxes and fines to the fledgling American government, some Friends continued to pay duties to England and were thus branded Tories and traitors to the American cause of freedom.

No longer in government themselves, Friends chose not to take disputes to courts of law, preferring arbitration within their Meetings. Happily, they did not withdraw altogether from public life. Rather, their missionary spirit was reinvested in campaigns against slavery and the slave trade, in the reform of prisons and asylums, in the construction of hospitals, and in increasing justice.

Early on, American Friends suffered from an ambivalence about education. Eventually they rectified it but too late to leave a significant mark on American culture. Harvard, Yale, and William & Mary colleges were founded as seminaries to support the ordained ministry of the established churches of their respective colonies. Ironically, when the College of Philadelphia (now the University of Pennsylvania) was founded, it was not by Quakers but by a coalition of Anglicans and Presbyterians.

Friends, of course, have no need of seminaries because they have no clergy. Moreover, as Rufus Jones explains, "the Quaker naturally and logically looked upon the true minister as a passive and oracular 'instrument' of the Holy Spirit . . . not a teacher or an interpreter [but] a revealer through whom Divine Truth was 'opened.'" George Fox had favored the creation of educational institutions to teach everything "civil and useful in the creation," but his followers were slow to comply, with the consequence that (in Jones's words) "no adequate education for Quaker youth was available [and] they soon found themselves largely cut off from the great currents of culture."

The problem was the early Friends' failure to regard the revelation of knowledge, either divine or human, as more than passive. Jones laments,

> Their failure to appreciate the importance of the fullest expansion of human personality by education is the primary cause of their larger failure to win the commanding place in American civilization.

William Penn himself demonstrated the early Quaker ambivalence toward learning. Although he possessed a substantial personal library, he famously warned his children to "have but few books," arguing that "more true knowledge comes by Meditation and just Reflection than by Reading; for much Reading is an Oppression of the Mind, and extinguishes the natural Candle; which is the Reason of so many senseless Scholars in the World."

Nevertheless, at the time of the Quaker abdication from government, Philadelphia was arguably the most civilized and cultured city in the new nation, boasting seventy-seven bookshops—second only to London in the English book trade. The Friends' religious tolerance welcomed peoples of many faiths, enriching the community. By 1759, Philadelphia had three Quaker meetings and two Presbyterian churches as well as a society of Freemasons and Lutheran, Dutch Calvinist, Swedish, and Roman Catholic churches, plus Anabaptist and Moravian meetinghouses.

If the Holy Experiment did not succeed in establishing Penn's vision of heaven on earth in the New World, it nevertheless demonstrated the civilizing tendencies that would combine to form the American character. The Declaration of Independence was conceived and published in Philadelphia, and the City of Brotherly Love became the first capital of a new nation conceived in liberty and dedicated to the proposition that all men are created equal with inalienable rights—surely articles of Quaker faith. The original Quaker-drafted constitution of Rhode Island became the model for the nation's Bill of Rights.

Quaker historian John Punshon notes that

> Pennsylvania became a beacon of hope for all who shared the Quakers' belief in equality and human dignity; the relations of the Commonwealth with the Indians redeemed in some small measure the many atrocities otherwise visited on the Native Americans; the penal code was unparalleled in its humanity at the time. Out of the vision of one man and his religious Society sprang an application of those principles that would soon lead to the creation of American democracy, and an assurance for lovers of freedom everywhere that their hope was not in vain.

In these important respects, despite Thomas Jefferson's disclaimers, William Penn's Holy Experiment was clearly a success from which every American since has benefited.

• 8 •

Living in the Light of Eternity

Neither death nor life . . . will be able to separate us from
the love that comes to us in Christ Jesus, our Lord.

—Romans 8:38–39

There were no clergy present when my wife's parents were buried because they were not churchgoers. So the family conducted the graveside
service on its own, relying on these and other words from the Book of
Common Prayer to affirm the perennial belief that death has no dominion over life.

Many of us, as we go through life, are ambivalent about death and
uncertain about an afterlife. Perhaps by dint of their simple living, Quakers tend to be long-lived. It is just as well because they are focused on
what can be savored and accomplished this side of eternity. They may be
vague about their expectations of eternal life, but they do not obsess
about sin and salvation, leaving the initiative to their creator.

Humankind's lingering ambivalence about life and death was most
famously expressed by William Shakespeare. Contemplating the remains
of his servant Yorik, Prince Hamlet asked, "To be, or not to be?" [as if
life and death were equal options!]

Quaker faith recognizes no such option. Friends do not choose between life and death but affirm life altogether—life past, present, future,
and eternal. As Jesus hung dying, he turned to his fellow convict and
promised, "Today you will be with me in Paradise." Friends quietly cherish the same promise.

Christian faith is based on trust that the creator of life will not allow it to be extinguished. St. Paul, who never knew Jesus in life,

87

acknowledged, "If Christ is not risen, then our faith is folly." Paul and most of his fellow apostles went to their deaths as martyrs to our faith in the firm hope of their Resurrection. Even today, 2,000 years later, many Christians conclude their prayers, "Forever and ever—Amen" to signify the expectation of never-ending life.

We have faith that death is not a period to be placed at the end of a sentence but merely a comma inserted between this life and the next. Accordingly, Quakers take a longer view of life: living now in the light of eternal life.

The certain prospect of eternal life alters everything in one's present life. Secular culture rests on the notion that each human being belongs to himself or herself and that the only evil is to do harm to another person. A secularist lives with the conceit that he is his own policeman, judge, and jury. By contrast, religious faith insists that we belong not to ourselves but to God and are responsible to our creator.

Quakers understand that this makes each of us morally responsible for ourselves as well as others and indeed for all of God's creation. The reality that we belong to God shifts the focus of our lives forward so that we experience the present life as a prelude to an eternity that consists of nothing less than intimacy with him, where love reigns as the only rule of life.

The columnist and novelist Anna Quindlen suggests that, for believer and unbeliever alike, the only realistic way to confront life is to consider it a terminal illness. We're all going to die eventually, she reckons, so we must live fully, investing all we can so that when we pass on to eternity we have much to take with us. Paul tells us that in heaven there are many mansions, but we can't wait until we arrive to build our eternal home. We need to build now. No one on his deathbed has ever complained that he didn't spend more time at the office. Anna Quindlen's father gave her this advice: "If you win the rat race, you're still a rat."

To be honest, many people look only as far ahead as the ends of their noses as they pursue goals they hope to realize in this life, not beyond it. Moreover, most believers assume that if they are not wicked, God will somehow take care of them when their earthly lives are over. To be sure, we haven't much of a notion about heaven, except those prayers that mention "eternal rest," which Emily Dickinson said reminded her of a pretty boring retirement.

The churches and the Quakers aren't much help either with details, and probably for good reason: if they speculate much on heaven, they can be accused of fantasizing. You'll notice, for example, that the Church doesn't have much to say about the near-death experiences that 25 million Americans claim to have had.

Psychologist Carl Jung expressed the conviction that this life is but an interval between two eternities. Like the poet Wordsworth and the Mormon founder Joseph Smith, Jung believed not only in an afterlife but also in preexistence. But to be clear: Christianity does not believe in the preexistence of any person except Jesus ("In the beginning was the Word").

Nor does Christianity believe in reincarnation (whereby we die, only to revive and start the same old life cycle again, utterly unaware of our previous lives). The faith holds that death is real and that it is natural and that it is only a pause in a life that has a beginning but will have no end.

On the death of parents, many people begin to feel like orphans, and they begin to think about their own mortality. That does not necessarily make them morbid. Polls reveal that only one-fourth of older Americans acknowledge fearing death. However, two-thirds of us admit to fearing pain, decrepitude, and the loneliness of lingering illness from which death is a deliverance. Unhappily, modern medicine tends to prolong life at the expense of the quality of life.

In reality, death is natural and inevitable. In centuries past, death came quickly, usually of infections and accidents. In our great grandparents' time, it was not uncommon for a person to be born, to give birth, and to die in the same bed. My wife recalls houses in her native Ohio that were built with a special door leading to the parlor just wide enough for a casket. It was opened only for wakes. Death then was greeted as natural.

Quakers, in the company of other Christians, affirm life. Christianity considers taking one's own life the most contemptible of sins—worse even than murder, which can be repented. To take one's own life is to reject the creator and to destroy his greatest gift—life itself.

Although life expectancy at birth is at an all-time high in America, life affirmation is not. We live in a suicidal society today, although our method of choice is typically subtle and even inadvertent, as increasing numbers of people abuse their health, inviting their own decline and premature death. Fully one-third of Americans are now obese, prone to heart disease, high blood pressure and cholesterol, and diabetes, the silent killer that leads to blindness, the loss of limbs and body functions, and early death. Ironically, in our land of plenty, the poor are more likely than the rich to be obese.

What information do we have about eternity? In the Gospel, we know that Jesus' friend Lazarus truly died, bringing Jesus to tears. When Jesus restored his friend to life, Lazarus had nothing to report about his experience, presumably because he had rested in "Sheol," the murky place that Jews assumed was the resting place of the dead. Possibly, Lazarus was only in some kind of suspended animation, not in eternity. But once Jesus rose from the dead, death lost its sting, and life became eternal—not as some kind of reward but simply as a matter of fact.

Abraham Lincoln warned that we cannot escape history. Jesus assures us that we cannot escape eternity either. That means that we must live now in the prospect that we will live forever with the God who made us, sustains us, and loves us. If we are destined to live with him forever, it is clearly not premature to make his acquaintance at the earliest opportunity—now. Years ago I wrote a popular book on preparing for eternity, proposing ten thoughts for pursuing our present lives in the light of our eternal destiny. Quakers would find them congenial:

1. Death doesn't hurt; life does.
2. You are not the first person to make this trip.
3. You *can* take it with you.
4. This trip is not a vacation.
5. You are not going somewhere, but to some*one*.
6. You are not prepared, but it doesn't matter.
7. Be prepared for surprises.
8. You are leaving nothing behind.
9. You have been preparing all your life for this.
10. Enter eternity laughing.

Quakers, I confess, are not renowned for humor, but they laugh a lot from sheer gratitude for life, for the sheer joy of being alive, and for the hope that life will never end.

By means of film and videotape, technology has already conferred a *virtual* immortality on persons who have long since departed this life. I have seen the Astaire–Rogers films countless times and reckon the dancing pair to be more alive than I often feel. Most of the recordings I enjoy are by artists who have long since gone to their reward. In the worlds of art and culture, no one need be lost to death.

Poets are counseled to die young, the better to be remembered for their youth and vitality. But Quakers hold that the fabric of life is all of one piece, now and hereafter, and is ageless. By living in the light of heaven, they believe we will enter eternity youthful and ready for adventure.

In the universe of the spirit, as in physics, nothing is ever lost; it is only transformed. The infinitesimal atom that is now compost in my garden may one day be in a brain cell of the next Einstein or the next saint. The lives we now lead—with whatever misgivings and handicaps—will never truly end. Instead, they will be merely transfigured.

Our deaths will make a difference, but they will not make *us* different. In eternity, it is fair to predict that we will be more ourselves than ever before. Were we funny in life? We will be hilarious in heaven. Were we terrors? We will be terrible in eternity.

As the economist John Maynard Keynes acknowledged, "In the long run we're all dead." Nevertheless, Quakers are persuaded that death does not end life but is only a transaction that will allow us to trade in aging old models for ones better equipped for eternity. It is a prospect to which we wisely devote our lives, helping us prepare for the final moments approaching eternity.

During the course of their lives, some farsighted Americans, seeking to spare their loved ones the expense of disposing of their mortal remains, arrange to purchase cemetery plots and headstones. Some even prepay the mortician for their final sweep from dust to dust. As the old saw affirms, the only sure things in this world are death and taxes, and while the taxman visits frequently, the Grim Reaper puts in but a single appearance. So one should be prepared, and Quakers aim to approach eternity with serenity.

When I was younger, I suspected those of my friends who turn first to the obituaries in the daily newspaper to possess a morbid streak. But their sheer numbers forced me to reconsider my judgment and to sneak a look myself at the death notices before concentrating on the sports, comics, and editorial pages.

Because of the pressure of deadlines and the unpredictability of events, journalism is a sometimes-slapdash enterprise. Practitioners like myself therefore produce prose that falls far short of literature. The notable exceptions are the largely anonymous worldwide corps of obituary writers who, as historians-before-the-fact, enjoy the leisure of assessing the lives of persons still living, in full confidence that the only flourishes they will need to add before their stories' appearance is a sentence about the time, place, and cause of the subject's death.

Compared to reporters who occasionally risk life and limb pursuing stories their editors may never run, obituary writers are confident that with patience (and in complete safety), their efforts will eventually see print.

Many years before Ronald Reagan breathed his last, an English friend of mine confided that he was the author of the obituary that would run in *The Independent* newspaper when our former president died. My friend continued to reshape and update the piece from time to time in heady confidence that, when the piece was printed, its subject would be in no position to object to anything in it.

In the better British newspapers, obituary writing has developed into something of an art form, celebrating lives rather than merely mourning their passing. The *Economist* notes that "obituary writers tend to be unhappy at even the suggestion that their work has anything to do with death as such—beyond its necessary role as a requirement for publication." A well-written obituary concentrates not on what the deceased left behind but on what he or she contributed in life. What each of us stands for and values in this life is what we will carry into the next.

Rabbi Harold Kushner has argued that the only permanent satisfaction acquisitiveness can offer is the possession of a life that has meaning. If there is any literal truth to the notion that heaven is a neighborhood composed of "many mansions," then each individual resident is architect, builder, and landscaper of his own heavenly housing. Eternity is not simply an extended run of the play we have been acting all our lives. Rather, it is our big chance: taking our act to the Great White Way. In eternity, our names will be in lights. The critical question remains, How good is our act? Far from being an indulgence of Walter Mittyish fantasies, our afterlife will be the realization of the realities we have valued and to which we have devoted ourselves in good times and bad this side of the Great Divide.

I suspect the afterlife is like a paid-up mortgage. We will still enjoy the same "house" with all its comforts and peculiarities, but now no one can evict us—the result of our years of investing in it. If God makes me welcome, I suspect that my own "mansion" in eternity will be as small or large and as well or poorly maintained as my life has been. To mix metaphors, if the world is our oyster, then we will not want for nourishment in eternity. If, on the other hand, we have huddled for security in lives no larger than the closet of our own tiny thoughts and feelings, we will likely find our accommodations in eternity equally cramped.

Until recently, obituary writers followed the dictum *De mortuis nihil nisi bonum* (Don't say anything about the dead unless you can say something good). This is not unlike the physician's Hippocratic oath, First do no harm. True to that constraint, obits in the past took the form of funeral elegies (e.g., "Although never one to suffer fools gladly, he was untiring in his charitable works, devotion to family, and love of animals").

What is fresh in contemporary journalism is that the "fools" the deceased suffered during life now demand their fifteen minutes of celebrity to let the world know what they thought of the pompous old boy or girl. The new rule is that the frankness of the appreciation should match but not exceed the candor with which the subject conducted himself or herself in life. If we are guarded persons in life, our privacy will probably be respected, but our demise may go unheralded.

Regardless of how we are remembered, we earn our salvation not by impressing anyone—be it God, the public, or even ourselves—but by devoting ourselves to values we can carry into eternity.

Our contemporary reluctance to appreciate the promise of eternity stems largely from an aversion to facing the fact of death—which perverts a natural process into something to be feared. The denial of death is a very recent phenomenon and not a good one. As a child raised in the ethnic neighborhoods of Chicago, I was accustomed to witnessing death in the stockyards and packinghouses. But my lingering recollection is of the funeral homes where we mourned the latest neighborhood patriarch or matriarch to have departed life.

In our predominantly immigrant neighborhood, three and sometimes four generations of the same family lived cramped together in the same apartments, and the dying were tended to at home rather than in hospitals and nursing homes. Therefore, death, when it came, was something that literally visited the home, and it was only natural that the Polish, Czech, and Irish families of my youth should hold wakes there. Caskets were open for viewing, and no one considered reducing grandpa's or grandma's body to ashes in an urn. While the surviving adults and children sorrowed over their loss, they treated death as a final rite of passage and a consummation of a life of fidelity, full of hope. No one dwelled on death; nothing about these solemn occasions was morbid. Everything was natural.

The fear of death is misplaced. One can be *anxious*, for example, about debt, illness, unemployment, or the loss of love, attractiveness, and reputation because (1) these misfortunes are unpredictable and (2) they are painful in anticipation as well as in experience. By contrast, death is certain, and it does not hurt.

The prospect of eternity is fulfillment, not loss. It is the living who sense loss when a loved one or leader dies. The cliché at every wake is the inevitable observation that the deceased "looks peaceful." It is a cliché precisely because it is true: the dead do not grieve at all and have only passed through death to new life. It is those of us who remain who grieve our loss.

More often than not, the dying are ready to die, whether they are accident victims, children with cancer, young people with AIDS, or the aged, whose tired bodies have long since lost their warranty. It is their loved ones who are not prepared to lose them. In *A Grief Observed*, C. S. Lewis poignantly chronicled the loss of his wife to cancer after a few brief years of marriage. The most optimistic of men, possessed of an ability to discern sense in tragedy and to rationalize absurdity, Lewis nevertheless found himself devastated by his personal loss. If you recall his story from the film *Shadowlands*, however, you will remember that his wife was actually prepared for death. She was true to her given name—Joy—to the end.

Of course, we are speaking only of death itself, not of dying, which can be a protracted, painful, and degrading process. When he was not yet sixty-five, my father was forced to retire because of the degenerating effects of arteriosclerosis. Over the final twenty-one years of his life, he progressively lost his mental and physical faculties. Death, when it finally visited him, was deliverance. So, too, was my mother's passing a few years later. The only child of blind parents, raised on public welfare and private charity, she became embittered when the golden years for which she had toiled turned to rust. She died, immobile and bedridden after a series of illnesses, persuaded that life had cheated her, yet confident of a better eternity.

One can live with dignity, but dying is seldom dignified.

The cloud that surrounds death is really the mystery of evil and, more precisely, the problem of pain. There is perhaps no satisfactory explanation for suffering, and an explanation is not really what we seek in any case. Those who employ the existence of suffering to deny God's existence seek only to avoid pain. When that proves impossible, they blame it on the creator.

It is people, not God, who inflict suffering on themselves and one another. Pain is also the side effect of tragic, unintended accidents. Unthinking nature, running its course like a steamroller, often leaves victims in its wake. Still, death, while occasionally tragic, is seldom catastrophic; most often, one's passing is simply a quiet domestic and private drama.

To confront death is to celebrate life; to dismiss dying is to sleep through life. Increasingly, death is the last thing we plan for. In northern Virginia, where I live, historic cemeteries are preserved for American Revolutionary and Civil War dead, but scant provision is made to establish resting places for people like you and me. The land is too valuable as prospective homesites for those still living to be set aside for the dead.

Those who recognize death as the portal to eternity will make it welcome, as Francis of Assisi did when he exclaimed, "Welcome, my sister Death." Or as Garvin, a twelve-year-old English boy who died of bone-marrow disease a few years ago, consoled his family, telling them that "dying is not really dying; it is just like opening an old door into a new room which is heaven."

It is easy to snicker at such speeches as so much brave banter better suited for Hollywood death scenes. In fact, it is only a recent development that survivors are expected to console the dying. The traditional expectation was just the other way around. Thomas More not only forgave his executioner but went to great lengths to lift the spirits of his family as he approached his end. To his daughter he wrote, "Never trouble thy mind for anything that ever shall keep me in this world," reminding her that "nothing can come but that which God wills."

While skeptics may be inclined to cling futilely to the present life for fear of the beyond, believers can make the opposite mistake of assessing their present lives as trivial compared to eternity. Both assessments are faulty. Life is but the curtain-raiser to a worthy play and death but a brief intermission. A good Act One establishes the plot, the pace and the characters for the rest of the play—and so with eternity.

After we die, the lives of most of us will be celebrated for but a generation by those who shared our table, our friendship, or our bed. But in the eternal scheme of things, we will be more than a memory: we will have made a mark for good or ill. And perhaps even the world will be better off for our brief sojourn here. George Eliot might have had us in mind when she wrote in *Middlemarch*,

> [The] growing good of the world is partly dependent on unhistoric acts; and that things are not so ill with you and me as they might have been is half owing to the number who lived faithfully a hidden life, and rest in unvisited tombs.

Those, like the Quakers, who live the present life in the light of eternity do not fear the Grim Reaper. Rather, like convivial pub dwellers who have had their fill, they are prepared to roll home when the proprietor announces, "Time, gentlemen, please!" If that simile strikes you as too secular and English, then exchange it for the graceful exit of old Simeon in the Gospel who, having held the infant Jesus in his arms (Luke 2:29–32), exclaimed, "At last, Lord, you can dismiss your servant in peace, as you promised. For with my eyes I have seen your salvation."

Quakers believe that life's greatest adventure is still ahead of each of us.

· 9 ·

Why Did the Quakers Stop Quaking?

I bid them tremble at the word of God.

—George Fox

$\mathcal{T}$he title of this chapter is not of my own invention. It was a question—a challenge, really—posed to me at the Chautauqua Institution in the first summer of the new millennium. I had been invited there to prognosticate publicly about the future of religious faith in America.

My challenger was a Pentecostal minister who was annoyed at my characterization of contemporary religious faith as fuzzy, personal, emotional, and largely insulated from the imperative to love God and serve one's neighbor. I was wearing my Quaker colors that week, so he was implying by his question that the Quakers of their founder's time were more like Pentecostals are today—fervent, emotional, evangelical, Christ centered, empowered by the Spirit, and devoted to mutual service. He was politely implying that contemporary Friends had lost the fervor of their forebears.

I'm not good at thinking on my feet, but I believe the response that popped into my head that day was pretty apt. I suggested to him that Quakers stopped quaking because we stopped being persecuted.

George Fox himself revealed why and when Quakers started quaking. "Justice Bennet of Derby was the first that called us Quakers," Fox recalled, "because I bid them tremble at the word of God. This was in 1650."

Like other reformers, Fox sought not to create a new faith but to restore the authentic faith and practice of the earliest Christians, whose pagan neighbors marveled, "How they love one another!" Of that original community of faith, the Acts of the Apostles relates, "There was complete agreement of heart and soul. . . . A wonderful spirit of generosity pervaded the whole fellowship. Indeed there was not a single person in need among them" (Acts 4:43–44).

In the three centuries before Christianity became the official faith of the Roman Empire, it was persecution that kept the community of faith bound in love and service. But when the Romans stopped feeding Christians to the lions and became believers themselves, the Church became increasingly complacent, casual, complex, and corrupt, not to mention impersonal.

In just the first decade of George Fox's ministry, some 60,000 men and women were converted to the restored faith, and Quaker missionaries risked death and imprisonment to persuade others to become Friends of the Truth. The first generations of Friends consciously took up the mission of the apostles, reflecting Jesus' command that "what is revealed to you in secret, preach from the house tops" (Matthew 10:26–27).

From the outset, Quaker missionaries sought to turn people "to that inward light, spirit, and grace by which all men might know their salvation, and their way to God." They preached in markets, at fairs, and in the streets—anywhere they could find a crowd—and alerted people to their need for repentance and conversion. They actively sought confrontation with authorities to dramatize the difference between active faith and mere complacency.

They became renowned for truth telling—something that did not endear them to their pious and self-satisfied contemporaries. Fox pleaded, "Be obedient to the Truth, and spread it abroad, which must go over all the world, to professors, Jews, Christians, and heathen, to answering the witness of God in them all."

The first generation of Friends took their faith to Ireland, France, Germany, Italy, Holland, Denmark, Surinam, Turkey, the West Indies, and the American colonies. William Penn said of them, "As they freely received what they had to say from the Lord, so they freely administered it to others. The bent and stress of their ministry was conversion to God, regeneration, and holiness."

The early Quakers quaked because God's light shone on their sins and shortcomings, and they took seriously Jesus' command in his Sermon on the Mount that we be perfect as our heavenly Father is perfect.

They called themselves Friends because Jesus told his followers, "You are my friends if you do whatsoever I command you" (John 15:14).

It was not at all the early Quakers' purpose to establish an alternative to the established Church but rather to purify the practice of religion. As Fox wrote, "None can make better than the pure undefiled religion, which was set up in the church in the apostles' days . . . unto which all that profess Christianity should be conformable."

Fox and his followers intended to convert the world to the restored faith. But today, centuries later, membership has shrunk to fewer than 17,000 Quakers in its country of origin, and missionary work has decreased dramatically. In the United States alone, it has taken fully three and a half centuries to double the numbers that embraced the Quaker faith in its first ten years.

Still, despite these disappointments, Friends today enjoy an impact and a reputation that far exceeds their numbers. As Robert Lawrence Smith writes, Quakerism has endured "because it so directly connects with our best instincts and highest aspirations . . . that all of us in this world are interdependent and must be responsible for each other."

G. K. Chesterton famously lamented that "Christianity has not been tried and found wanting. It has been found to be difficult and has yet to be tried." But Quakers still do try. Friends recognize that idealism is hollow unless they "try what love can do" by making peace, achieving true equality, and creating a more humane society. They act on the principle that every man, woman, and child shares the same humanity, the same indwelling God, and an inner guiding light. As Friends of the Truth, they are committed to plain speaking rather than political correctness, confident that the truth will make the whole world free.

Although many reject their underlying pacifism, they applaud Friends' commitment to peacemaking and honor it. To this day, the American Friends Service Committee and its British counterpart are the only religiously affiliated organizations in the world to have been awarded the Nobel Peace Prize (1947). When conflicts arise among nations and peoples around the world, Quakers are there not to proselytize but to provide relief. Unlike other relief organizations, they remain long after immediate needs are met to help with conflict resolution and to restore community.

Here again, Quakers are distinctive: they do not takes sides in conflicts because they respect the common humanity among antagonists whom they mean to help.

Given these affirmations about the vitality of contemporary Quakerism, I nevertheless express what Friends quaintly call a "concern"—namely, that Friends' declining numbers may be attributed to a waning in their ability to articulate precisely what they believe as Quakers, which hampers their ability to witness to the truth.

Much as they treasure silent worship, it's worth pondering whether, over the years, Friends may have become too quiet for one another's good, let alone for the good of those outside our fellowship. Silent worship is an invitation to God to reveal himself to Friends as a community. But silence in at least some meetings may reflect an inability to share their faith with one another or to commit themselves to something more than lives of searching after truth as their holy grail.

Granted, all serious persons are pilgrims in search of truth, but at some point we are wise to cease from spiritual seeking to acknowledge that the Good Shepherd has already found us. And we must reflect that, although God's revelation is continuous, enough has already been revealed for us to live confidently and effectively in faith, hope, and love.

It will be objected that the faith of Quakers cannot be put into words—at least not into a formal creed. Still, the Inner Light shines on *something*, piercing through our ignorance. It reveals something—and it must be the *same* something for everyone to affirm a common faith as Friends of the Light.

The early Quaker missionaries were required to articulate their faith in some detail. I often wonder what Friends would say if they were required, like Mormons and Jehovah's Witnesses, to go door-to-door (like Jesus' disciples) to share their faith with strangers and convince them of its truth.

Even if birthright and convinced members could articulate the faith that still binds them as Friends, what do the great number of casual attenders at Quaker meetings hold in common? Why are so many content to remain in a kind of religious limbo, ever searching but not committing themselves? In many Friends meetings, visitors outnumber members, reminiscent of tourists meandering through the dusty cathedrals of Europe, while worshippers have shrunk to a virtual handful.

The Quaker mantra is humble—that one must wait patiently and expectantly to be led. But their Quaker forebears felt impelled to articulate their faith and share their convincement. They were not reluctant, nor were they dilettantes. Rather, they quaked because they trembled at the word of God.

Today, Friends' abhorrence of credal religion is an unfortunate invitation to sidestep positions on some moral issues that engage and divide other Americans of faith. What is the Quaker stand on abortion, euthanasia, embryonic research, and genetic engineering, let alone on drug control, divorce, contraception, and premarital sex? I would submit that there is no consensus, so the subjects are left to the politicians and the secular society.

It is common among contemporary Friends to pride themselves on not needing a creed. But Fox had no hesitation in articulating his faith. Consider his letter to Friends of February 4, 1685:

> There is one God, the creator of all, and one Lord Jesus Christ, by whom all things were made and created, who is the one mediator betwixt God and man; even the man Christ Jesus; there is one body, and one spirit, even as you are called to one hope of your calling; and one God and Father of all, who is above you all, and in you all, and through you all; and there is one faith which Christ Jesus is the author and finisher of; and there is one baptism, and by one spirit we are all baptized into one body, whether we be Jews or Gentiles, bond or free, must all drink into this one spirit of Christ, and so to keep the unity in the spirit, which is the bond of peace. For the apostle saith, "If any man have not the spirit of Christ, he is none of his" (Romans 8:9).

Fox's mission was based on his faith: "I was to bring people off from all their own ways to Christ, the new and living way . . . to the Church in God, the general assembly in heaven, which Christ is the head of. . . . And I was to bring people off from all the world's religions, which are vain . . ."

To be sure, turning to the Light was never pleasant because it revealed one's shortcomings, whereas the Quaker preference today is to think well of everyone. But John Punshon notes about the early Friends, "This was the point at which one quaked with fear at the power of God. It was the religious experience that gave the Friends their name:

> There are not many lights, but only one. . . . The doctrine of the Light was a doctrine of the real presence of Christ . . . capable of generating the same power and conviction. . . . Membership . . . meant involvement in this spiritual warfare against economic, social, and religious evils. You needed to have a convincement that endured,

but also a willingness to be enlisted in what they called "The Lamb's War."

Nearly one-half of American Protestants claim to have had a "born-again" experience they describe as a saving encounter with Jesus, which has led them to accept him as their personal Savior. As I've noted, few contemporary Quakers either seek or will admit to such an experience. In its place, most cherish a quiet shared mysticism. Spoken testimonies aside, few of them are either able or willing to share with one another what they experience in their silent worship together.

The great mystics of all faiths took pains to describe their experiences so that others not so blessed might be more confident in their faith. Here is what Blaise Pascal wrote of his experience:

> Fire . . . the God of Abraham, Isaac, and Jacob. . . . Certainty, certainty, emotion, joy, peace, the God of Jesus Christ. Thy God shall be my God. Oblivion of the world and everything except God. Joy, Joy, Joy, tears of Joy!

Now that's inspiration! Should any contemporary Friends chance to have an experience anything like that, I pray that they will not keep it to themselves but rise in their meetings and prophesy. They will all be better Friends of the Truth for the sharing. But at times when Quakers are not feeling inspired at all, they still need to affirm a common faith that binds them together as Friends of the Truth.

John Punshon is but one of many distinguished Friends who believe Quakers have misplaced some of their original inspiration as a community. He notes that "there are quarters where Christianity is seen as an option for Quakers as a matter of personal choice but in no sense part of the corporate testimony of our Society. . . . In place of Friends' traditional doctrines and ways of discerning guidance, many modern Quakers take the view . . . that the essence of Quakerism . . . is that it has no doctrines." The Quaker historian agrees that "in spite of wide variations of belief, Friends share many common values" but insists that "I go to meeting to worship God, not to have values. Most of my values come from somewhere else."

British Quaker Alistair Heron worries that "in 30 years' time the membership of the Society will need to be described by terms such as ethical, humanist, secular. By then only a minority will affirm personal experience of the living power of the Spirit of God in their daily lives." He asks, Are we a *religious* society or merely a *friendly* society? He laments that "there is no systematic provision of Quaker or biblical teaching" in contemporary Quakerism and that "many of those regularly attending meeting for worship can do so for years without learning much about the Quaker heritage of faith.

"Certainly few newcomers unfamiliar with the Bible (or the New Testament) can expect to remedy that situation by attending a Quaker meeting for worship. . . ." Moreover, there is typically only one Quaker in a household, so mutual support in faith is absent within the family. Revealingly, as recently as 1998, there were only eight marriages between Quakers in all of Great Britain.

Woodbrooke College is a kind of Quaker think tank in England. In 1980, Joan Fitch, a fellow at Woodbrooke, made "an attempt to find out why present-day Quakers seem unable to state our faith convincingly to the world, just at a time when it is desperately needed." She admitted that "the main drift of what is said [in meetings for worship] will be of a liberal, kindly, non-committal sentiment."

She concluded with this mixed portrait: "How do I see the Society of Friends here and now? I see us as a small body: quiet, sober, respected, aging, middle-class, compassionate, incorruptible, usually liberal, but rarely radical."

In her 1997 Swarthmore Lecture, Christine Trevett noted that increased liberalism and individualism among Friends had created a "culture of silence" in respect to articulating and transmitting Quaker faith and values. She writes, "I found myself asking myself more urgently whether Quakerism knew what it was," adding, "If there is any agreement worth a mention about what we stand for . . . we must ensure that it is understood by those who wish to be part of us and are part of us. This is not credalism. This is taking seriously the validity of our corporate leadings, and the experience of our history."

America's founding psychologist William James noted in his classic text *The Varieties of Religious Experience*,

> The Quaker religion which Fox founded is something which it is impossible to over-praise. In a day of shams it was a religion of veracity rooted in spiritual inwardness, and a return to something more like the original Gospel truth than men had known . . .

In my wife's and my experience, Quakers are among the most generous people in the world. Friends owe it to God and to one another to articulate their common faith and individual enlightenment. Because they dispense with clericalism, all Quakers are required to minister to everyone. Who knows? If they can manage that, they might start quaking again and shake up the rest of humankind.

After I shared these thoughts to an audience at Guilford College, a Quaker in his eighties stood to give this testimony.

He said, "I know why I don't quake: I don't ask God the hard questions about what he requires me to do with my life. I'm afraid that if I ask him, God will tell me something difficult that I'm unwilling to do. But if I was willing to listen to him, and do what he demands, then I'd start quaking."

· *10* ·

A Peculiar People

Quaker meeting has begun,
No more laughing, no more fun,
If you chance to crack a smile,
You will have to walk a mile.

—Anonymous

If your acquaintance with Quakers before opening this book was limited to the smiling man on the oatmeal box, you are not alone.

Until I reached retirement age, the Society of Friends was a mystery to me as well. Apart from the Quaker Oats man, my sole point of reference was the film *Friendly Persuasion*, in which Gary Cooper played the role of a Quaker farmer at a time when our nation was younger and simpler.

But I was aware that two of my favorite novelists, Jan de Hartog and James Michener, were outspoken Friends, so there had to be something to commend the Quaker way of life to persons who were so wise in the ways of the world as well as the spirit.

As children, my wife and her friends used to recite the doggerel that depicts Quaker life as "no more laughing, no more fun." Without giving it much thought, I assumed that Friends were humorless, abstemious, and given to quaint speech and dress. In the film, Gary Cooper wore even simpler clothing than the Quaker Oats man and addressed everyone as "thee" and "thou."

Even now, I won't dispute the popular preconceptions altogether but only affirm that the quaintness that survives among Quakers in the twenty-first century possesses both a certain charm and a great practicality. Friends' ways are endearing because they are enduring. Their sense of humor stems from their optimism and realism. Cognizant of the pre-tensions to which human nature is prone, Quakers are quick to laugh at their own foibles.

Were they a more numerous sect, they might attract more detrac-tors. Instead, Friends are mostly overlooked, which is okay with them because they do not proselytize. But occasionally they are the butt of jokes. The Hampstead meeting on London's periphery counts celebrities such as Dame Judi Dench as members. A sign out front reads, "Welcome to the Society of Friends." With a keen sense of mischief vandals have scratched out the "r" in "Friends," leaving passersby with the impression that they are being welcomed by *Fiends*!

Moreover, some readers of my syndicated column inadvertently misspell the word Quaker as "Quacker"—as in duck or goose. Alas, in my youth, Catholics used to be derided as "mackerel snappers," so reli-gion appears to be a perennial equal opportunity employer of aspiring humorists. No matter.

Quakers are known popularly as "peculiar people"—a sobriquet they accept with equanimity. To be sure, few of them dress like the Quaker Oats man, although my wife and I know a couple that dons "plain dress" every day, looking for all the world like Grant Wood's *Amer-ican Gothic*, as they ride his-and-hers motorcycles cross-country during the warmer months of the year.

When Friends worship or just gather socially, the dress code is sim-ply "come as you are" as opposed to Sunday best. The underlying idea is that God created us naked and remains unimpressed by fashion. Our Quaker meeting in Virginia tends to attract homeless people, not least because we offer free lunch to all comers. Often, I can't distinguish members from vagrants by the clothing they wear, only by their hygiene.

Friends compensate for their lack of a rite of Penance by two means: The reading of "Advices and Queries" and "Eldering."

The former consists of admonitions, typically in the form of ques-tions. Here are a few examples.

Are you open to the healing of God's love? Do you try to set aside times of quiet for openness to the Holy Spirit? Are you following Jesus' example of love in action? Do you work gladly with other religious groups in the pursuit of common goals? Be honest with yourself. What unpalatable truths might you be evading? Do you respect that of God in everyone though it may be expressed in unfamiliar ways or be difficult to discern? Do you cherish your friendships, so that they grow in depth and understanding and mutual respect? When decisions have to be made, are you ready to join with others in seeking clearness, asking for God's guidance and offering counsel to one another? Are you honest and truthful in all you say and do? If pressure is brought upon you to lower your standard of integrity, are you prepared to resist it?"

That may strike you as nagging, but Friends aren't expected to defend themselves against the queries—only meditate on them.

Every now and then, a member will interrupt silent worship with a query that other Friends suspect reflects a personal agenda and is just a form of nagging. Members who are too free with their personal opinions are "eldered"—that is, privately confronted with their prejudices by seasoned Friends and reminded of the need for mutual respect. That remedy tends to quiet those who prefer to preach and argue a point to a captive, silent audience.

Friends meet monthly after worship to transact business, which concerns everyone in a congregation that has neither clergy nor paid employees. Business meetings are considered extensions of worship and called Meetings for Worship with a Concern for Business. In business as well as other aspects of life, Quakers wait to be led by the Spirit to make decisions. Majority votes are insufficient; neither is an overwhelming consensus of those present. Nothing is decided without unanimity.

As a consequence, meetings are slow to act and inclined to wait and see. The stables adjoining our Virginia meetinghouse are partially collapsed and have been propped up by beams for years, waiting for the meeting's clear "leading" about what to do about them.

To be sure, there are queries that justify inaction: "Do we humbly set aside our own preconceived notions as to proper action, seeking instead Divine guidance as to the right course?" "Is the Meeting aware that it speaks not only through its actions but also through its failure to act?"

A certain latitude for eccentricity among Quakers is tolerated and even welcomed. Some otherwise inspired members are disinclined altogether to give oral testimony. Yet others can be long-winded and occasionally incoherent. We've had a few members who rise to *sing* a sentiment: not a hymn, mind you, but possibly something from the Lerner & Lowe songbook. Occasionally someone just stands and weeps loudly.

Because Quakers possess a tradition but no creed and because they hold God's revelation to be open ended, spoken testimony tends to be personal rather than biblically oriented, occasionally sounding more like New Age than Christian thinking, and we are treated to quotes from the Buddha, Lao Tse, Kahlil Gibran, and even Mohammed. Friends are fond of the truth but not discriminating as to its sources.

Some testimony is less enlightening than it is an expression of the speaker's uncertainties. Sometimes it is sentimental but heartfelt all the same. We are not shy about speaking up and asking Friends to hold sick or troubled loved ones "in the Light" and then reporting on their progress at the next meeting—all in the spirit of an extended family. Meetings are sufficiently small that everyone turns up for a wedding or a memorial service. As I've noted, everyone in attendance signs the marriage certificate as witness to a loving contract.

Beyond their silence, simplicity, social service, sexual equality, and radical democracy, Quakers are peculiar in three ways: their dedication to truth telling, peacemaking, and opposition to the death penalty. They take seriously the Mosaic commandment to refrain from swearing oaths on the basis that everyone has the responsibility to tell the truth without swearing on the Bible. Civil courts in the United States accede to this reluctance, so that now those testifying in court merely *promise* to tell the truth, the whole truth, and nothing but the truth, without the need to invoke God as witness to their integrity.

The requirement that they be peacemakers is derived from the Sermon on the Mount. For many Friends this is translated into pacifism, such that some Quakers refuse to register for the military at age eighteen, and others withhold that portion of their taxes that are destined for military purposes. Registering as a conscientious objector to war is a bit onerous but not impossible, but evading taxes is something else altogether. In the past some pacifist Friends have emigrated to small countries with insignificant military capabilities. Most stay at home and are active in antiwar protests, most recently against the war in Iraq.

Before dismissing them as impractical ideologues, it's wise to remember that Quakers were awarded the Nobel Peace Prize after World War II, not for being obstructionists but for their work in European reconstruction and conflict resolution. What all Quakers share is an aversion to violence. Most of them see the value of police and other security forces that deter violence and maintain the peace. They acknowledge that one can defend oneself or loved ones from violence but without resorting to physical violence themselves.

Despite their modest numbers, Quakers are in the forefront of opposition to the death penalty in the United States. In this respect they are less controversial. European nations have largely repealed the death penalty, and the Catholic Church believes it should be considered only as a rare exception. The rationale, of course, is that the state has no more right to take a life than a criminal does. God gives life; for the state to take it away is revenge, an ancient prohibition.

American Quakers have a particular interest in supporting Native Americans—a practice that dates from William Penn's Pennsylvania. They do not proselytize but simply support poor Indian communities. Through the American Friends Service Committee, Quakers collaborate with much larger church-related service agencies and the Red Cross to aid the victims of war and natural tragedies.

Precisely because their capabilities are limited, Friends tend to specialize in assistance. In Kosovo they provided games and Frisbees for children in refugee camps and helped rebuild public libraries in war-torn communities. Quakers tend to remain in disaster zones and communities long after large aid agencies leave, concentrating on conflict resolution. A Quaker aid official to whom my wife was an adviser used to sign his letters "Peace and Bread"—indicative of Friends' priorities worldwide.

Individual meetings relate to either the Friends General Conference (FGC), headquartered in Philadelphia, or the Friends United Meeting (FUM), based in Richmond, Indiana. Those affiliated with FGC adhere to strictly "unprogrammed" silent worship; those belonging to FUM combine silence with scriptural readings, music, and homilies in their worship and even enjoy the service of ministers.

Red-state and blue-state Quakers tend to diverge on their politics, like other Americans. For example, FGC Friends are more inclined to welcome gays and those raised in non-Christian faiths as members, and they are more supportive of pro-choice feminism and vocal in support of environmentalism. That said, all Quakers adhere to the essentials of common faith, practice, and tolerance, whatever their individual political predilections.

Just as it is possible to be at one and the same time a Pentecostal Christian and an adherent of a mainstream Protestant denomination—or a Roman Catholic for that matter—it is possible to live, act, and worship as a Friend while still holding to the faith in which one was born and raised. Quakerism is neither a church nor a sect but a way of life.

That is why many Jews, Muslims, Buddhists, as well as Christians are attracted to it without thereby denying their fundamental faiths and identities. I was born, raised, and educated through theological school as a Catholic and have rejected none of that legacy. The truths all Christians hold in common form the foundation of my faith and make demands on my conscience.

It was my wife, raised without religious faith, who was first attracted to the Friends, not least because they were unencumbered by dogma and institutional trappings. I joined her enthusiastically, without abandoning anything I had formerly believed, and we are a better couple for that mutual decision.

Friends not only attract men and women grounded in other faiths who find Quaker practice compatible with those faiths. They also attract those who are seekers after the truth, many of whom traditionalists like myself might be tempted to dismiss as agnostics or even atheists. Traditional Christianity holds that God has always assumed the initiative in revealing himself to us, needing only to be accepted and listened to, not sought and found. In the ages of faith everyone was familiar with God's initiatives, but we live today in a lost-and-found world.

In modern times many sincere men and women have lost the ability to tune in to God's promptings, yet they sense a void in their lives that can be filled only by something or someone greater than themselves. Jesus himself urged his followers to "knock and the door will be opened to you; seek and you will find" (Matthew 7:7). For those still seeking, Friends have a friendly door on which to knock.

Get a group of Quakers to start talking about God, and God himself may have trouble recognizing himself in the discussion. Whereas Jesus promised that "wherever two or three are gathered in my name, there I am in the midst of them" (Matthew 18:20), Friends patiently acknowledge that whenever two or three Quakers get together, there may be five different opinions.

On one thing all Friends agree. In the words of George Fox, "Let your lives speak," a reiteration of Jesus' wisdom about people that "by their fruits you shall know them." The Quaker faith is one of experience and effort rather than speculation. Friends are tested by action.

After the early flowering of the Quaker movement, Friends abandoned proselytism for teaching by example. So rest assured, Quakers will not knock on your door, bombard you with leaflets, harangue you on television, or otherwise campaign for evangelization. They are not impressed by numbers, only by authentic living. They leave to God himself the job of leading us. But should your curiosity ever get the best of you, you will find them quietly welcoming, as friends who—like you—are sons and daughters of God.

Since this is a chapter about Quakers as Peculiar People, let me leave you with a final, outrageous peculiarity of Friends: they are not interested in your money. At our meeting there are no Sunday collections, only an occasional appeal for some charity everyone has agreed on, and an opportunity to bring food for our poor neighbors. Indeed, the only time the subject of money is brought up is toward the end of the year, when we balance free-will donations and income from old legacies against our expenses for the year just ending.

I suppose no one should be surprised that worshipping in a simple manner requires so little money. I can't speak for all Quaker meetings, but our plain old meetinghouse has long since been paid for, and there are no salaries to cover, just our utilities, the occasional repair we can't manage ourselves, and some luncheon supplies not covered by potluck offerings. Our fairly substantial library consists largely of books donated over the years. My wife and I do the meeting's shopping along with our own every week at a wholesale discount store, buying paper towels by the dozens and paper cups by the gross.

We get by with electric space heaters in the winter, huddling for warmth, and lack air conditioning altogether. There are no building campaigns. I have always admired Christians who tithe their congregations based on their income. To commit a substantial percentage of one's income to one's church is not only a sign of generosity but a spur to commitment. In our case we encourage Friends to contribute directly to society's needs.

If you are intrigued by the possibility of sharing your own peculiarities, you will find a quiet welcome and a home away from home with Friends, who will not ask you to abandon your own faith or doubts but merely discover a simple and satisfying way to worship the God who dwells in all of us.

But don't let me influence you; it's best to leave it to God to lead.

• 11 •

What Jesus Learned in the Desert and Thoreau Learned in the Woods

Teach us to care, and not to care. Teach us to sit still.

—T. S. Eliot

All human evil comes from this: man's being unable to sit still in a room.

—Pascal

*S*itting still in a bare room is something Quakers quickly learn to do, sharing their solitude and silence with one another in expectation of Jesus' promise that wherever two or three of us are gathered in his name, he is there with us.

To be sure, I have not the slightest notion what is going on in the minds of my fellow Friends as we sit quietly for an hour of a Sunday. I suspect that not much is going on at all or, rather, that we all have calmed down sufficiently from the previous week's concerns to be receptive and perceptive. Emptying one's mind leaves it open, liberated from one's own parochial preoccupations, and ready to be occupied with something better.

In silence we attempt to emulate Jesus of Nazareth who, at the age of thirty, entered the desert alone to fast and pray, then emerged to begin a brief public ministry that ended with his death. There is no reason to believe that Jesus spent his time in the desert in deep depression, focused on death. To the contrary, his retreat focused on life and affirmed that there is no cause for despair and every reason for hope, that God's kingdom was at hand and that he would proclaim it.

Because Christianity affirms that Jesus is divine, we tend to assume that he could read minds and the future and that he knew absolutely everything from the outset, even as a babe in the manger. That assumption opens a needless chasm between him and us and makes it impossible to comprehend and appreciate him. Although Jesus identified himself with his Father, Jesus was also clearly and fully human, unlike his Father. It is pointless to speculate how Jesus' humanity and divinity coexisted and combined in practice, but it is critical to remember that he was fully human like ourselves. Whereas God does not sleep, Jesus did. God does not pray, but Jesus did. God does not weep or become weary or hungry, sweat blood, or feel pain and betrayal. God does not die, but Jesus did all these things.

We know from the Gospel account that, when Jesus was twelve, his parents lost track of him in Jerusalem, only to find him studying with the scholars in the Temple. We can assume that he had to learn carpentry from Joseph. The Scriptures tell us that he grew in wisdom and grace.

Quakers believe that if the Son of God could grow in wisdom and grace, so can we all.

What did Jesus learn during his desert sojourn? And what can we learn from his experience? The Gospels tell us he was hungry and that he was tempted to pride and ambition. Satan literally offered him the world, and he refused. Precisely because the forty days and nights alone were an ordeal for Jesus, he learned from his lengthy retreat to be constant and faithful, dutiful, dedicated, caring, and hopeful. Of course, it was in his character to possess these virtues, but his ordeal confirmed them.

Strictly speaking, Jesus was not alone in the desert. His Father was there with him, and there were no distractions from prayer. That is something we share with him when we are silent.

Consider another celebrated retreat into silence and solitude. In the spring of 1845, a young American, Henry David Thoreau, went into the Massachusetts woods and, with a borrowed axe, made himself a home on the shore of Walden Pond, where he lived alone for two years and two months. "My purpose in going to Walden Pond," he explained, "was not to live cheaply nor to live dearly there, but to transact some private business with the fewest obstacles."

That "private business" was to learn about himself. The purpose of his adventure was to establish his own values and agenda rather than pattern his life according to others' expectations of him. Thoreau believed that, by thoughtless conformity, the majority of men and women "begin digging their graves as soon as they are born."

Thoreau prefaced the account of his sojourn in the woods by acknowledging that "I should not talk so much about myself if there were anybody else whom I knew as well." He was a fortunate man to possess such self-knowledge, which only increased.

Among the "difficult sayings" of Jesus are those in which he insisted (like Thoreau after him) that his followers break away from the familiar and routine. To the rich young man of the Gospel, Jesus said, "There is one thing you still need. Go and sell everything you have, give the money away to the poor. And then come back and follow me" (Mark 10:21).

In the next breath he assured his followers that "nobody has left home or brothers or sisters or mother or father or children or land for my sake and the gospel's without getting back a hundred times over" (Mark 10:29–30).

As you and I grow older, we can no longer navigate the years remaining to us by following the paths of our youth. Instead we must march, in Thoreau's imagery, to a different drummer—and we are that drummer. "Our life is frittered away by details," Thoreau lamented in his retreat as he distanced himself from cares inflicted on him by others. "The mass of men lead lives of quiet desperation," he said.

We retreat into silence and solitude not to escape living but to ensure that we will return to our lives as more autonomous and involved persons. Jesus went into the desert for forty days and nights, then rejoined life with a clear mission. Mohammed went to the mountain, only to return transformed. Prince Siddartha retreated from life, only to find the wisdom to lead others to serenity as the Buddha. Thoreau himself became "a sojourner in civilized life again" after twenty-six months in the woods to share his wisdom with the rest of us.

Thoreau was anything but pious. Urged by his friends to prepare his soul for the next life, he complained to them, "One world at a time!" He died prematurely at the age of forty-five. Not unlike Jesus, who also died a young man, Thoreau packed more experience and appreciation into his short life than most of us. Typically, we are cautioned to become more philosophical as the years pass. But being philosophical can mean being resigned to fate, reducing our expectations, and investing in security rather than fulfillment. Of course, everyone experiences good and ill fortune during the course of their lives, but our destinies are not writ in the stars. Accidents and coincidences unpredictably help or hinder us, but only we can plot our lives and choose what to pursue, be it accomplishment or enjoyment.

We are, if not quite masters of our fate, yet rich in hope because we are God's own creatures, made in his image to enjoy his company eternally. So, instead of being philosophical, we would be better advised to becoming *theological*—to see ourselves from our designer's perspective. While our bodies age, our souls are ever immune from the ravages of time. Just as God never ages, our spirits are forever young. We are never too old to grow young in spirit.

When G. K. Chesterton each summer sought out vacation lodgings for his family near the sea, he did not inquire of his prospective landlady how often she changed her lodgers' bedding or how well she fed them. Such an inquiry, he sensed, would be not only impolite but counterproductive.

Instead, the impish Chesterton inquired of his prospective hostess, "Madam, what is your theology of the universe?" The pundit reasoned that if the landlady believed in an orderly universe filled with hope and trusted a generous God to love his creatures and treat them equitably, then she would most likely provide clean bed linen and satisfying meals to her guests.

The creator who made us in his likeness is forever young. Calling on his grace, we can *grow* young as the years pass, and we can find a richness in life that eluded us in our youth. A wise bishop once noted that God has much more on his mind than religion. He is the author of all that exists, so life itself in its fullness is his preoccupation.

If our todays and tomorrows are only repetitions of our yesterdays, we are not living as well as we might. As we age, our lives should expand and our spirits grow.

Christians who pray for "eternal rest" at life's end, I suspect, have never really lived. As a child, I was taught that this world is a "vale of tears," to be stoically endured until happily exchanged for eternal bliss. To be sure, too many lives are vales of tears. In the Third World, for example, 24,000 men, women, and children die each day from starvation alone. They have good reason to think of death as deliverance. But we who live in the developed world do not.

Whatever heaven is like, it will not be a retirement community. In eternity we will not trade in tired old personalities for something better. Rather, we will be the identical persons, somehow glorified and purified, but the same nonetheless. So what we make of ourselves this side of paradise is what will determine the eternities we enjoy. If we lack a sense of humor now, we can't expect to acquire one in heaven. If we fail to smell the roses now, there will be no flowers gracing our paradise.

Too many people reach the end of their lives regretting having missed what might have been. "I could have been a contender," they insist, but they gave up the fight long before the bell. George Eliot had the better wisdom: "It's never too late to be what you might have been." Oscar Wilde, confined to a prison workhouse, discovered that "the final mystery is oneself." That is the mystery you and I have time to solve, in silence and solitude, with God's grace to help us.

Something is wrong with our concept of Christianity if it seems arrogant to identify ourselves with Jesus. That is exactly what he intends us to do. The essence of Christianity is the imitation of Christ.

Whether baptized in infancy or as adults, Christians believe they have died to their worst selves and have been reborn into the better selves God had in mind when he first conceived of creatures made in his image and likeness. But they must affirm that new life. Some Quakers never undergo formal baptism but make the same life affirmation.

The greatest compliment anyone can receive is that the world became a better place because he or she graced our planet and shared our lives. For Quakers and all Christians, Jesus is our role model. The Jesus of the Gospels is not enigmatic. We know the following:

- How he treated parents, friends, enemies, officials, women, children, strangers, the rich, the poor, and sinners
- How he acted when confronted by treachery
- How he handled emotion
- When he spoke and when he kept his peace
- When he celebrated and when he denied himself
- How he prayed and what he prayed for
- What he valued and what he despised
- How he regarded violence
- How he loved

- What he thought was worth a miracle
- What he thought was worth dying for

Jesus died a young man but packed a lot of living into his brief years. In silence and solitude Quakers and non-Quakers alike can reorient ourselves to the fullness of life that comes from imitating him.

To See the World in a Grain of Sand

To see a world in a grain of sand
and a heaven in a wild flower
hold infinity in the palm of your hand
and eternity in an hour

—William Blake

The poet's aspirations are worthy of our consideration in silence and solitude. They are achievable this side of paradise if we keep active, reverent, and appreciative. There will always be time for long thoughts and even longer loves if we will but take the time. All we require is to share the Quakers' inclination to silently ponder and to care.

Even as our physical eyesight falters, our spiritual insight can grow. If we will but take the time, we can see a world in a grain of sand and a heaven in a wildflower. God has always held the whole world in his hand. If we will but extend our own hands, we can touch the border of infinity. If we will live fully in the present moment—without regret for the past or anxiety for the future—we can contain eternity in an hour.

The confidence we need to navigate the autumn and winter of our lives flows from faith in ourselves, which begins with self-knowledge. "Explore thyself!" Thoreau urges us all. Shakespeare's Hamlet marveled at the human animal:

What a piece of work is man! How noble in reason! How infinite in faculty! in form and loving how express and admirable! in action how like an angel! in apprehension how like a god! the beauty of the world! the paragon of animals!

Yet in the next breath, the prince's faith in man and himself faltered:

> And yet, to me, [Hamlet asked] what is this quintessence of dust?

Hamlet's faith in man and himself lacked hope and love. As the years pass we will want to nurture a faith that secures our future and engages our affections as well as our minds. For that we need a faith in something—or someone—beyond ourselves.

And we need the silence and solitude to grow into that faith.

If we conceive of ourselves as mere accidental specks of life in a vast, impersonal universe, we are not likely to entertain a faith that holds out much hope. Believers and doubters are equally exposed to life's trials, but believers know where they stand in the universe and where they are going.

In both the first and the final analysis, no one can live free of faith. If you or I attempted to live confidently on the basis of what we know for an absolute fact, we could never get out of bed in the morning to face the uncertain day. While people cannot help but live by faiths that fall short of certitude, we can shed patently false faiths that are built of little more than habit and sentiment, and we can build a faith full of hope.

In silence and solitude, consider your faith, starting with what you believe about yourself. What kind of person do you think you are? Then ask yourself what you do daily to justify your faith in yourself. For example, if I consider yourself a truthful person, what hard truths have I revealed or confronted lately? If I fancy myself as being generous, what acts of kindness have I displayed of late? Next consider: What do I believe in *beyond* myself? In what—or whom—do I place my faith? To be worthy of adherence, my faith needs to be bigger and better than I am.

Francis of Assisi was once challenged by a peasant who had heard of the friar's generosity. The simple man advised the saint, "Try to be as good as people think you are." From all reports, Francis succeeded. Despite a life of almost inconceivable deprivation and generosity, no happier man ever lived.

Although Quakers, like all Christians, operate on faith rather than mere instinct, they must beware of becoming the slaves of their beliefs. Much of the world's misery comes from people who devote themselves wholeheartedly to causes supposedly "greater than themselves." Let's save the whales if we can, but let's save our marriages, our families, and our own lives first and keep faith with our fellow man and our creator.

Quakers are naturally suspicious of idols and ideologies, aware that most people find it easier to have faith in a crusade than to believe in themselves. Devoting ourselves to causes can make us feel good about ourselves because they lift us above our loneliness and petty concerns. But every crusade can leave victims in its wake because of the righteous fervor of its adherents.

The allure of idolatry is as ancient as humankind. The Israelites found it easier to worship a golden calf than their invisible and demanding God. Be warned: only God is worthy of being idolized. Idolatry of anything less is evasive; to prevail throughout life, we need to revere the real thing.

In the twentieth century, more than 100 million men, women, and children died miserably and prematurely in time of war—the victims of faiths that converted their adherents into self-righteous killers. By contrast, a good faith is not cocksure but honest and humble, generous and true. A worthy faith takes no prisoners and claims no victims. Among the great religious faiths, Christianity has endured because it is based on generosity, love, and forgiveness and the creator's own sacrifice for us. That is a common object of meditation among Friends.

In his Declaration of Independence, Thomas Jefferson inadvertently misled us: happiness is not an objective to be pursued by divine right. Rather, scientists have confirmed that joy is a by-product of an engaged life. Contented people do not pause to ask themselves, "Am I happy yet?" They are too preoccupied doing whatever it is that occupies their attention—whether it be work or family or hobby or simply doing good for others. Through some still-elusive chemistry, bringing joy to others makes us happy as well.

I'm old enough to be listed in *Who's Who in America*. There you will find statistics, such as my birthplace and date, the names of my wife and children, the schools I attended, the jobs I've held, awards I've won, and titles of books I've written to date. But nowhere will you find a mention of my faith or values—whether I'm a coward or a cad, generous or stingy, attentive or preoccupied, gregarious or friendless, or whether I possess a sense of humor. It is chilling to acknowledge that when I die, some anonymous obituary writer will borrow from that meager entry to summarize the significance of my life.

Sometime during your life you probably composed a résumé that was just as inadequate to describe who you were then and are now. I suggest you choose an epitaph for yourself before someone else chooses it for you. It is a mistake to leave it to others to take the measure of your life after you are gone. But it will take silence and solitude for you to meditate on the meaning of your life.

Many celebrated men and women are careful to write their memoirs to cast themselves in the most favorable light and head off revisionists who think less of them than they do of themselves. A noteworthy exception was Jesus of Nazareth, who wrote nothing about himself and left it to his friends to tell us who he was. But Jesus knew himself and what his life was about. To live fully and die well, we must reflect on who we are, what we stand for, and how we relate to our creator. It's never too soon to write your epitaph.

"But my life is not over," you may object. "How can I take the measure of it?" To which I answer: by that time it will be too late. Writing your epitaph is an exercise in separating what is important from what is merely ephemeral, then projecting your true values to the end of your life. Although the creator gave us life, it is we who create its shape and give it direction. Our power of creativity is our likeness to God.

When at the end of your days this side of eternity a eulogist or obituary writer composes an appreciation of your life, what do you want it to say? Look back over your life and acknowledge your accomplishments and failures, your aspirations and satisfactions, and recall the people who were important to you. Compose it, as Quakers do, in silence and solitude. If you choose to preserve it on paper, it can serve as the script for the rest of your life. Without that script, you will be unable to appreciate the gifts you have already been given and those that will bring you the greatest joy as you approach the frontier of eternity.

On our travels, my wife and I have toured old cemeteries in Britain and America, touched by the sentiments carved on crumbling stone by survivors who not only grieved but celebrated the lives of the deceased. In these peaceful places lie not just human remains but "devoted husbands," "faithful wives," and "cherished children." The sentiments make the difference and they are full of hope. Consider these lines carved in the headstone of a young man who died of yellow fever in New Orleans more than a century and a half ago:

> But why indulge these notes of grief,
> Why should we thus complain?

> What now to us is less severe
> Is his eternal gain.

When, at length, Henry David Thoreau abandoned his solitary life at Walden Pond, he gave this explanation:

> I left the woods for as good a reason as I went there. . . . I had several more lives to live, and could not spare any more time for that one. It is remarkable how easily and insensibly we fall into a particular route, and make a beaten track for ourselves.

The hermit of Walden returned to society but carried Walden's wisdom with him the rest of his life:

> I learned this, at least, in my experiment: that if one advances confidently in the direction of his dreams, and endeavors to live the life which he has imagined, he will meet with a success unexpected in common hours. He will put some things behind, will pass an invisible boundary; new, universal, and more liberal laws will begin to establish themselves around and within him.

But that revelation requires human investment:

> In proportion as he simplifies his life, the laws of the universe will appear less complex, and solitude will not be solitude, nor poverty poverty, nor weakness weakness. If you have built castles in the air, your work need not be lost; that is where they should be. Now put the foundations under them.

"Love your life," Thoreau urges us. "Meet it and live it; do not shun it and call it hard names. . . . The fault-finder will find faults even in paradise.

"Things do not change; we change. Sell your clothes and keep your thoughts. God will see that you do not want society. If I were confined to a corner of a garret all my days, like a spider, the world would be just as large to me while I had my thoughts about me."

Thoreau related a story about an artist who devoted his life to striving after perfection, only to find eternity:

> His singleness of purpose and resolution, and his elevated piety, endowed him, without his knowledge, with perennial youth. As he made no compromise with Time, Time kept out of his way . . .

Quakers possess no patent on silence and solitude and the riches that meditation can confer. We can all devote ourselves to the adventure of living, now and forever, bearing in mind Thoreau's counsel that "only that day dawns to which we are awake. There is more day to dawn. The sun is but a morning star."

Conclusion

How the Quakers Are Reinventing America

The wolf shall dwell with the lamb,
And the leopard shall lie down with the kid;
And the calf and the young lion and the fatling together;
And a little child shall lead them.

—Isaiah 11:6

$\mathscr{I}$t is the supreme irony that, having succeeded in persuading their fellow Americans of their values of freedom, tolerance, and human dignity, Friends then retreated from influence in the years following the American Revolution to pursue their own interests, shrinking in numbers as well. Because many contemporary Friends are loath to proselytize, preferring to rely on God's leadings, there are only about 206,000 Friends in America today.

The decline was probably predictable, considering that the Pennsylvania Quakers had already abandoned politics rather than defend their colony by armed force. After the new American nation declared its independence from Britain, its autonomy could be achieved only by a call to arms.

At the time of the Declaration, the population of the colonies was divided in its sympathies. Roughly one-third of Americans actively rallied to arms and the cause of independence. Another one-third continued to sympathize with the mother country, while the remainder sat on the sidelines during the conflict.

With the exception of freedom fighters such as Thomas Paine and General Greene, a majority of Quakers could not bring themselves to participate actively in the war for independence. Some even sought refuge in the British-held garrison cities and towns during the conflict, presuming king and parliament would prevail when hostilities ceased. At war's end, thousands of nonviolent Friends found themselves condemned as collaborators and traitors and fled the fledgling United States to make permanent homes in Canada. As early as 1777, forty Quakers had been arrested in Philadelphia; half were imprisoned. In Virginia, seven Quakers were cast into the wilderness during the dead of winter to expire.

RETREAT AND RECOVERY

Those Friends who remained in the new republic felt marginalized. Not only had they lost political influence, but the old evangelical spirit of George Fox had waned, and American Quakers retreated into quietism, tending to their own business, resting content as a modest minority within the expanding society, dealing kindly with their neighbors, and pursuing their values among themselves.

Further diluting their influence, Quakers soon split into factions, mimicking the Founding Fathers, who had formed competing political parties. For the Quakers, the schism tended to separate city and country Friends. In 1806, Philadelphia Yearly Meeting, in an attempt to tighten discipline, disowned any Friend who denied the divinity of Christ, the immediate revelation of the Holy Spirit, and the authenticity of the Bible. Others clung totally to the saving power of individual revelation, deemphasizing Scripture, Jesus' atonement, and his dual identity as man and God.

Contemporary American Quakers are roughly divided between the two emphases, but in practice all American Friends not only cooperate but also collaborate with one another.

No longer a force to be reckoned with by dint of their diminished membership and political power, Quakers continued to produce extraordinary men and women who revived the role of shaping the American character and influencing American life. It is not an exaggeration to credit Quakers with influencing the nation's conscience to abolish slavery, deal fairly with Native Americans, give women the vote, extend civil rights, preserve the environment, protect animals, and create a humane prison system aimed at rehabilitation rather than pure punishment.

Despite their small numbers, American Quakers were awarded the Nobel Peace Prize for their work in European reconstruction following World War II. They continue to pursue their humanitarian work world-wide in the twenty-first century. Over time they have created world-class schools and colleges, setting educational standards that persuade non-Quaker students to honor their humane values. Friends' spirituality increasingly resonates with Americans of all faiths and none.

To be sure, America has not quite caught up with its Quakers because American Friends continue to press for values and freedoms the larger society is not yet prepared to embrace—abolition of the death penalty, for example, and the promotion of gay and reproductive rights. But Friends are effectively organized to make a difference, with an active presence at the United Nations and on Capitol Hill and a powerful humanitarian relief organization that operates worldwide.

All of this was anticipated in the ministry of a single unassuming man who lived and died even before the American Revolution began. His name was John Woolman.

JOHN WOOLMAN AND THE ABOLITION OF SLAVERY

Anyone who aspires to write about Quakers is at an immediate disadvantage because Friends are not self-promoters. Indeed, they are notorious in their preference for anonymity. Until I became a Quaker myself, I knew nothing about John Woolman (1720–1772) despite his prominence as an early abolitionist and promoter of animal rights in America. Were Quakers inclined to canonize saints, Woolman would be the first to be so recognized. In my old set of the fifty volumes of the Harvard Classics Library, Woolman's *Journal* has the honor of being included in the initial volume.

The man who began his career as bookkeeper in a general store in Mount Holly, New Jersey, died at the age of fifty-one in York, England, having spent nearly three months walking all the way from London, proceeding by stages and stopping to speak to Quaker meetings along the way. To protest the inhumane treatment of horses, he refused to take a stage coach, nor would he mail a letter to be carried by coach.

After arriving in the old walled city, he fell ill of smallpox and died far from his native America. But before leaving London for York, he had already persuaded the British Quakers that slavery was contrary to Christianity and should be abolished. Earlier he had persuaded American Friends of the evil of slavery.

On a recent visit to York, my wife and I sought Woolman's grave in an old Quaker cemetery outside the ancient Roman walls, only to locate it in an adjacent yard behind new condominium apartments. The worn headstone was obscured by trees and brambles, the grave clearly unvisited.

Woolman's final journey capped a lifetime of walks throughout the American colonies devoted to persuading his fellow Quakers face-to-face to grant freedom to their slaves. The earliest Friends in America trafficked in slaves as commonly as their fellow colonists. But as early as 1671, George Fox, visiting Barbados, witnessed for the first time the actual treatment of slaves and protested that servitude was incompatible with Quaker values.

In 1742, while clerking in a general store in New Jersey, the young Woolman was asked by his employer to make out a bill of sale for a female slave to a fellow Quaker. Out of respect to his employer and the purchaser, he did so but was so troubled in conscience that he devoted the remainder of his life to abolishing human servitude as harmful to both slave and owner.

During his lifetime, one by one, the various Yearly Meetings of Friends proclaimed that emancipation was a religious duty. Within twenty years of Woolman's death in 1772, the practice of slavery had ceased among colonial Friends. His influence on animal rights would await the movement that originated with English Quaker Anna Sewell, whose book *Black Beauty* became a perennial best-seller condemning the inhumane treatment of domesticated animals.

Woolman summed up his life's mission as an attempt to ameliorate the unnecessary sufferings of humankind. It is a mission to which subsequent generations of Quakers have lent their efforts. In 1841, Eliza and Nathaniel Barney, prominent Quakers, organized the first antislavery convention in Nantucket.

During the run-up to the Civil War, Levi Coffin (1798–1877) and fellow Quakers were instrumental in creating and operating the celebrated Underground Railroad, which helped fugitive slaves to escape their masters and make their way through fourteen northern states to freedom in Canada. Quaker "conductors" hid the slaves in their homes and passed them along to Friends and other abolitionists farther north. As many as 100,000 slaves achieved their freedom through the involvement of individual Friends prior to Emancipation. Coffin, known as "president" of the Railroad, harbored 3,000 runaway slaves in his Newport, Indiana, home on their perilous journey to freedom.

QUAKERS AND HUMAN RIGHTS

Lamentably, emancipation fell short of guaranteeing black Americans the same rights as whites. Nearly a century would pass before Martin Luther King Jr. spurred a successful civil rights movement based on nonviolent protest. Dr. King's spiritual mentor was Howard Thurman (1900–1981), a fellow student of King's father. After being ordained as a Baptist minister in 1925, Thurman became the protégé of Quaker philosopher Rufus Jones at Haverford College in Pennsylvania.

From Jones and from travels that included conversations with Mahatma Gandhi, Thurman became persuaded that American blacks could achieve their full freedom of opportunity only through nonviolent protest. In 1953, Thurman became the first African American dean of chapel at predominantly white Boston University. He also established the first racially integrated, intercultural church in America, the Church for the Fellowship.

Thurman preached, "Don't ask yourself what the world needs. Ask yourself what makes you come alive and then go do that. Because what the world needs is people who have come alive." In his book *Jesus and the Disinherited*, he wrote,

> The religion of Jesus says to the disinherited: "Love your enemy. Take the initiative in seeking ways by which you can have the experience of a common sharing of mutual worth and value. It may be hazardous, but you must do it."

Martin Luther King Jr.'s dream was a Quaker dream based on the conviction that there is that of God in every person regardless of race, culture, gender, or faith. In 1964 the Quakers nominated Dr. King for the Nobel Peace Prize. Ironically, Dr. King's death provoked violence across the nation. Quakers successfully defused violent confrontations, helping to return the fight for civil rights to its nonviolent roots. Bayard Rustin, a lifelong Quaker, made nonviolence his mission.

As far back as colonial times Quakers had dealt with Native Americans as equals, purchasing land at a fair price from the Indians instead of taking it from them. To this day, Friends work on Indian reservations to ensure that Native Americans have advocates in Washington and the state capitals.

When the Prince Edward County, Virginia, public schools were closed to defy the U.S. Supreme Court's desegregation order in *Brown v. Board of Education* (1954), the Quakers' American Friends Service Committee (AFSC) placed African American students from the county with host families across the United States to continue their education. That move had been anticipated earlier when Quakers responded to the internment of Japanese American families during World War II by placing children of interns in colleges and finding work and lodging for their parents nearby.

Long before the civil rights movement of the 1960s, Quakers had identified racism as a leading cause of injustice in America. Crystal Bird Fauset, the first black woman to be elected to a U.S. state legislature, toiled for the Quaker relief service in the 1920s.

Although many contemporary Quakers are ambivalent about gay marriage, they actively support the lesbian, gay, bisexual, and transgender communities in seeking tolerance and equal rights.

SUSAN B. ANTHONY AND WOMAN SUFFRAGE

The extension of voting rights to American women was the work of many Americans in the nineteenth and early twentieth centuries. But its success as a movement cannot be conceived apart from the leadership of Susan B. Anthony (1820–1906), who was born and raised and who died a Quaker and who sacrificed marriage and family life to ensure voting rights for women. Like Moses long before her, she did not live to reach her goal. But her successor at the National Woman Suffrage Association, the Quaker Carrie Chapman Catt, lived to see passage of the Nineteenth Amendment to the Constitution, which became law in 1920.

Born and raised in Adams, Massachusetts, to loving parents, Susan remained close to her six brothers and sisters all her life. But as a child, she witnessed women's lives as drudgery and powerlessness. When Susan's mother was left an inheritance by her own mother, the law of the land forbade a married woman from receiving a legacy. American women were, in effect, the legal property of their husbands. That fact figured into young Susan's lifelong decision not to marry.

Young single women of the time fared little better than their married sisters. Susan's father opened the Anthony home to eleven teenage girls working in his mill to help support their parents and siblings. At the time, over two-thirds of mill workers in America were young single women, earning a pittance yet enjoying a measure of financial independence denied their mothers. The girls' example inspired Susan to seek full economic and political rights for her gender. From 1854 until her death, Susan B. Anthony devoted her life totally to women's rights.

Her motivation was religious, reflecting the Quaker belief that there is that of God in every person regardless of gender. Accordingly, every person deserves an equal measure of respect. When asked, "Do you pray?" she replied, "I pray every single second of my life, not on my knees, but with my work. . . . Work and worship are one with me." She credited her Quaker faith for her "radical egalitarianism." For Susan, faith in action was the only effective religion.

When she was sent in her teens to a Quaker boarding school in Pennsylvania, Susan found herself miserable away from home. But a meeting at the school with the celebrated Quaker abolitionist Lucretia Mott persuaded her of her own life's mission. Still in her twenties, Susan became the head of a girls school near Seneca Falls, New York, then joined the temperance movement and, in 1849, made her first public speech for the Daughters of Temperance. From the outset, the movement empowered women by offering them a public forum and affording them a reason to leave their homes without a male escort.

In 1851, Susan met both Elizabeth Cady Stanton and Frederick Douglass. Three years earlier at the Seneca Falls convention, Stanton, the mother of seven children, began a movement to champion the rights of women. She and Susan became fast friends and lifelong allies. Understandably, Douglass's first priority was the abolition of black slavery.

In 1852, Susan attempted to address a temperance meeting in Rochester, New York, but was dragged away by the men, who told her that "the sisters" are not invited to speak but "to listen and learn" from men. The same year she formed a delegation of women to address a hearing of the New York legislature aimed at closing loopholes in the trafficking of alcohol. It was the first occasion on which women addressed a legislative body with their own concerns. But Susan was again pulled from the podium when she attempted to address a temperance conclave. Shortly thereafter, she demanded and exercised her right to speak at a New York State teachers convention.

During the Civil War the fight for women's rights was obscured by the achievement of Emancipation. With the Thirteenth Amendment to the Constitution, slavery was abolished, but the Fourteenth Amendment limited the right to vote to black males. Susan felt betrayed by both Frederick Douglass and Horace Greeley, who reneged on their earlier support of universal suffrage. Then, in 1869, the Fifteenth Amendment affirmed the right of all citizens to vote regardless of race, color, or condition of previous servitude but still excluded women as though they did not qualify as American citizens. So Susan turned to lobbying for women state by state, traveling across America.

In 1872 she and Stanton proclaimed that marriage was a secular institution and that women had a right to divorce their husbands and gain custody of their children. That same year she registered to vote in Rochester, New York, and was arrested. When she attempted to take the case to the U.S. Supreme Court, her petition was denied.

Still, even during her lifetime, she enjoyed success. By 1896 women were enfranchised in four western states—Wyoming, Colorado, Utah, and Idaho. Many more trades and professions were open to them. They could keep the money they earned. Colleges and universities that heretofore were restricted to men opened to them, and common law marriage, which unfairly favored men, was annulled.

She campaigned in the United States and in Europe until her death at the age of eighty-six, repeating her motto, "Failure is impossible."

PRISON REFORM

Just as Susan B. Anthony was honored by being depicted on the American silver dollar, the Quaker Elizabeth Fry (1780–1845) is remembered on every five-pound note in Great Britain—the only woman other than the queen to be so remembered. It was Fry who successfully promoted the humane treatment of criminals in civilized nations. Modern penology in the United States reflects her concern for the rehabilitation of prisoners over their mere incarceration and punishment.

After John Randolph, U.S. envoy to England, visited Newgate Prison in 1819, where Mrs. Fry instituted her first reforms, he commented, "I have seen Elizabeth Fry in Newgate and I have witnessed there miraculous effects of true Christianity upon the most depraved of human beings."

The preference for imprisonment as punishment for crime is relatively modern. Until late in the eighteenth century, prisons held mostly debtors and those awaiting trial or execution. Conditions of incarceration at the time were appalling. Sanitation was practically nonexistent. At Newgate, Mrs. Fry found 300 women and their children huddled together in two wards and two cells, sleeping on the hard floor without nightclothes or bedding. The younger prisoners were at the mercy of rapacious jailers.

Over time—and against the warden's wishes—she provided the inmates with clothing and established a prison school and chapel, ensuring that female matrons replaced male guards. She also instituted a work program whereby the prisoners could sew and keep a portion of their earnings. Moreover, prisoners were given the opportunity to set their own rules within Newgate's walls.

In colonial Pennsylvania, William Penn anticipated Mrs. Fry's reforms by making imprisonment an opportunity for the criminal to experience a change of heart before being released back into society. Unfortunately, many prisoners were placed in solitary confinement with only a Bible to read, with the result that some actually went mad because of the isolation, even though their incarceration was otherwise humane and sanitary.

During her lifetime, Elizabeth Fry was unsuccessful in having capital punishment abolished, but she did achieve a reduction in the numbers and kinds of crimes that merited execution. She was enthusiastically invited by many nations to reform their prisons.

Today in America, over two million men and women are behind bars, straining the physical capacity of our prisons, which have largely abandoned efforts to rehabilitate criminals, concentrating instead on punishment. In 1971 the AFSC faulted the nation's criminal justice system: "Instead of promoting rehabilitation, the . . . system promotes inhumanity, discrimination, hypocrisy, and a sense of injustice." Today Quakers urge alternatives to imprisonment, including fines, restitution, reparation, and community service.

The disproportionate number of Americans imprisoned for drug possession has prompted proposals to offer treatment for addiction within the community and to require it for offenders.

By the same token, drunk driving is increasingly combated by disqualifying offenders altogether from driving. White-collar criminals and corrupt politicians can be disqualified from returning to their professions. Abusive parents can be deprived of authority over their children. Quakers, who invented modern penology, are now leaders in finding better alternatives to pure punishment.

A prominent Quaker criminologist is Doris Layton MacKenzie of the University of Maryland. She serves as codirector of the International Prison Project and testifies before the Congress and the United Nations on effective criminal justice. At the behest of Congress in 1997, she and her colleagues conducted for Congress a nationwide assessment of which measures actually work in corrections.

Programs that focus on punishment, deterrence, and control were discovered to be ineffective. These include correctional boot camps, arrests for domestic violence, house arrest, electronic monitoring, and intensive supervision of parolees. Talk therapy for sex offenders and residential treatment of juvenile offenders also rarely prove effective.

Programs that are effective in reducing recidivism include academic and vocational education in prison, courts specializing in drug offenses that mandate testing and treatment, behavioral modification for sex offenders, and cognitive behavior treatment. This involves restructuring the mental and moral perspectives that lend themselves to criminal behavior. Historically, the penitentiary received its name because it was intended to be a place that encourages penitence—a change of heart in the offender. Contemporary Quakers continue to work toward that end.

QUAKERS AND HUMANE EDUCATION

What do humorists Dave Barry and Chevy Chase have in common with novelist Frank Conroy, artist Maxfield Parrish, media mogul Norman Pearlstein, news anchor Charles Gibson, aviator Charles Lindbergh, acerbic author Gore Vidal, and former First Lady Nancy Reagan? And what do those notable Americans share with the children of Presidents Hoover, Nixon, and Clinton?

They are, all of them, products of Quaker schools in America.

You will recall that Quaker founder George Fox believed the universities of his time failed to equip Englishmen and women for real life instead cosseting them in sterile scholarship. And William Penn warned that the education of the mind alone could starve the spirit. While education was universal in colonial Pennsylvania, it was inclined to be practical.

Most early colleges in America began as seminaries for the education of clergy. Since the Quakers had no need for clergy, Pennsylvania left it to a combination of Anglicans and Presbyterians to create the college that is now the University of Pennsylvania.

American Friends soon compensated for their early ambivalence about formal education. They founded Cornell and Johns Hopkins universities, as well as Haverford, Swarthmore, Guilford, Earlham, Whittier, and other colleges. In addition, there are scores of Quaker elementary, prep, and boarding schools, open to all students who can qualify academically. Most students attracted to them are not Quakers.

Haverford College's motto reveals what Quaker education has always hoped to achieve in its students: "Not more learned, but steeped in a better learning."—*better* in the sense of being rigorous, humane, and comprehensive. Quaker schools do not yield to parental pressures to inflate grades; there are few straight-A students in them. At highly competitive Haverford, for example, the average cumulative grade point average is 3.3—a B+.

Quaker schools require their students to treat one another respectfully and to acknowledge their own dignity as children of the same God. Eschewing dogmas and creeds, they require tolerance, trust, openness and egalitarianism, instilling a thirst for genuine inquiry of mind and heart. Discipline, while firm, is based neither on regimentation nor on fear of punishment. The entire educational experience is aimed at richness of life and development of character and mutual service.

Quaker education in America was enriched by the innovations of Quaker schoolmaster Joseph Lancaster (1778–1838), who was born in London and ended his life in New York. At the age of twenty, Lancaster opened a free school in London and soon had over 1,000 students. By 1811, he had educated 7,000 children, not one of whom felt compelled to become a Quaker—a tribute to his disdain for proselytism. He held that schools could convey Christian values without being doctrinaire and sectarian. Refusing to resort to corporal punishment, he devised ways to appeal to the consciences of unruly and poorly performing students.

Despite the patronage of wealthy Quakers and others, Lancaster was always in debt (and once imprisoned for it) yet continued to create literally scores of free schools in England, Venezuela, Canada, and the United States.

One of the most celebrated of Quaker educators in recent times was John R. Coleman, an economist who served as longtime president of Haverford College. To underscore his conviction that education encompasses experience as well as academic study, Coleman assumed the identity of a poor itinerant laborer, working incognito at blue-collar minimum-wage jobs throughout the American South. In his book *Blue-Collar Journal*, he chronicled his experience as a homeless man working by the sweat of his brow.

In 1930 on a property adjacent to Pennsylvania's Swarthmore College, Quakers created Pendle Hill, a year-round community for education and spiritual growth that to this day welcomes anyone seeking enlightenment and a respite from secular routines. It was named for the peak in England's Pennines where George Fox experienced his conversion. Like most Americans, Quakers are too individualistic to be attracted to utopian monastic communities, but they accept that people learn best from one another and that religious faith is tested in the rough-and-tumble of confronting the personalities and needs of others.

MODERN QUAKER WRITERS IN AMERICA

Thomas Paine, raised a Quaker, famously proclaimed, "My mind is my own church," trusting his own intelligence, experience, and inspiration over dogma and institutions. Paine's attitude is shared by many (if not most) Americans today.

"In the late 17th century," Daniel J. Boorstin reflected, "Quakerism had many qualities which would have suited it to become the dominant American religion"—at once a communal and individualistic faith, tolerant, optimistic, and activist. That Quakerism failed to achieve its promise can be laid to a number of factors. American Friends actively sought persecution, retreated from politics, and embraced the idea of being "peculiar"—a people apart, converting their antipathy to dogma into a kind of dogma. In Boorstin's words, "Quakerism—traditionally form-less, spontaneous, and universal—built a wall around itself, [becoming] one of the greatest lost opportunities in all American history."

But the original Quaker spirit continues to resonate with the American character. Although the overwhelming majority of Americans continue to believe in God, pray regularly, and identify a religious pref-erence, only a shrinking minority worships together regularly. Religious life in twenty-first century America, whether fervent or lackadaisical, has become almost exclusively private and personal. It actively looks for in-spiration, which has always been a Quaker specialty.

Friends are not preachers, but they do write. During the first fifty years of the Quaker movement, 650 Friends (including eighty-two women) published more than 3,100 titles. It is through their writing that contemporary Quaker authors have chosen to foster a spirituality that springs from experience and resonates in twenty-first century America. J. Brent Bill, long associated with the Earlham School of Religion, in-cluded me in his *Imagination and Spirit*, a compilation of extracts from the writing of fifteen contemporary Quaker authors of drama, fiction and nonfiction alike.

Here is how Bill characterizes the lessons that emerge from their writing:

> That God speaks directly to the individual; that each individual has worth, dignity, freedom, and responsibility before God; that the Gospel is rooted in peacemaking and love; that there is that of God in every person; that God's will can be known and obeyed; that faith involves an immediate personal encounter with God; that commun-ion with God is intimately related to our inner spiritual experience; that moral purity, integrity, honesty, simplicity, and humility are es-sential to the Christian life; that Christian love and goodwill are ways of life that overcome hatred and violence; that Christ-like love finds expression in humanitarian service and social justice; that the Spirit of God grants us insight, guidance, and understanding of spir-itual truth; and that our faith and our life's practices must be mar-ried. Probably the three best-known Quaker writers are James Michener, Jan de Hartog, and Jessamyn West, with Phil Gulley the relative newcomer. West and Gulley write about Friends, but Mich-ener and de Hartog are more circumspect about revealing the source of their values.

Michener is best known for his epic novels that chronicle the moral struggles of Americans. In his *Chesapeake,* he offered a fictionalized account of the 1659 execution of Quakers on the Boston Common. One of the condemned men described his faith as "the simple discovery that each man is his own pathway to God." Before he died in 1997 at the age of ninety, Michener had given away everything he owned other than the clothes on his back.

Jan de Hartog, born in the Netherlands, was a leader of the Dutch Resistance to the Nazis in World War II. Smuggled to England, he later settled in Pennsylvania. You may recall his poignant play about marriage, *The Fourposter,* later made into a musical titled *I Do, I Do.* His novel *The Captain* evoked the terrors and moral dilemmas faced by the commander of a seagoing tugboat in enemy-infested waters. Later, he wrote a Quaker trilogy, including *The Lamb's War.*

Jessamyn West, born in a Quaker community in Jennings County, Indiana, taught in a one-room schoolhouse. An invalid much of her life, she died of tuberculosis in 1984, but not before winning an Academy Award for her screenplay of *Friendly Persuasion,* adapted from her book of the same title. The film provided Gary Cooper with perhaps his most memorable role—as a Quaker farmer chafing at the restrictions of his chosen faith.

Philip Gulley, born in 1961, is a prolific author of homespun tales that combine truth and fiction in a manner reminiscent of Garrison Keillor. Gulley's first effort, *Front Porch Tales,* sold a third of a million copies. He couches his Quaker values in stories of the challenges faced daily by ordinary people. Here is a little wisdom imparted in his essay *For Everything a Season*:

> Ultimately, to be grown up means that wisdom, reason, and love dictate our choices, as opposed to emotions, lusts, and urges. . . . If we allow ourselves to hate other persons and make choices on the basis of hate, rather than on the basis of wisdom, reason, and love, we are not grown-up. For we are allowing our emotions and urges to dictate our actions. Grown-ups don't do that; children do.

Quakers don't have theologians, but they do have popular philosophers who specialize in spirituality. Elton Trueblood (1900–1994) was widely acclaimed as the "dean of religious writing" in America during his productive years. He taught at Guilford and Haverford, served nine years as chaplain at Stanford, then completed his long career at Earlham, pausing for a period of public service with the U.S. Information Agency in Washington, D.C.

Trueblood called for all Christians to meet the challenge of their faith and to act as ministers. He lamented that Americans of goodwill shy from real Christianity. In *The Incendiary Fellowship*, he wrote that good people

> who constitute the obvious majority, are almost universally opposed to the kind of Christianity represented in the New Testament. The claims are too strong; the price is too high; the fire of evangelism is too hot. The crucial fact is that all evangelism is faintly embarrassing. . . . Though the New Testament describes a hot fire, we prefer the damp wick.

Thomas R. Kelly (1893–1941) taught philosophy at Earlham, Wellesley, and Haverford colleges and took up the same theme. In *A Testament of Devotion*, he argued that for the Christian

> no average goodness will do, no measuring of our lives by our fellows, but only a relentless, inexorable divine standard. No relatives suffice; only absolutes satisfy the soul committed to holy obedience. Absolute honest, absolute gentleness, absolute self-control, unwearied patience and thoughtfulness in the midst of the raveling friction of home and office and school and shop.

Douglas Steere (1901–1995), a prolific writer on spiritual themes, spent most of his teaching career at Haverford but also taught at Union Theological Seminary in New York. He helped organize the Quaker Relief Action Group following World War II and served as president of the American Theological Society. In *Dimensions of Prayer*, he affirmed that

> Christian prayer brings a relentless clarity. But underneath its fierce realism and its costly baptism of personal responsibility, there is an equally steadying sense that in whatever we are called to do, we do not work alone, and that in spite of the lump of sin that is all too apparent, there is a great legacy of good to be drawn upon in mankind. Chain reactions of goodness may be released that carry immeasurable power.

Arguably, Richard J. Foster, a lifelong Friend, is Steere's heir in articulating the Quaker spirit. But Foster is better known as an advocate of mainstream Christian spirituality. He was a founder of Renovaré, an ecumenical fellowship "committed to working for the renewal of the Church of Jesus Christ in all her multifaceted expressions." Perhaps Foster's best-known work is *Celebrations of Discipline*, in which he argues,

> Superficiality is the curse of our age. The doctrine of instant satisfaction is a primary spiritual problem. . . . The classical Disciplines of the spiritual life call us to move beyond surface livings into the depths. They invite us to explore the inner caverns of the spiritual realm. They urge us to be the answer to a hollow world. . . . Leo Tolstoy observes, "Everybody thinks of changing humanity and nobody thinks of changing himself." Let us be among those who believe that the inner transformation of our lives is a goal worthy of our best effort.

TRANSLATING INSPIRATION INTO ACTION

It would be a mistake to think that contemporary Friends sit silently waiting for the inspiration of the Spirit. Their success as activists on the national and international stage belies their modest numbers. In this work they engage other Americans of goodwill and continue to inspire the best in the American character.

Although Rufus Jones (1863–1948) was widely acclaimed during his lifetime as the preeminent American Quaker philosopher, historian, and spiritual writer, he was also an indefatigable leader and organizer, ensuring that Friends effectively influence public policy in the United States and provide humanitarian aid around the world.

In 1917 the AFSC was created, building on humanitarian work Jones had instigated. It provided on-site relief services during the years following World War I. Jones served for twenty years as the AFSC's chairman. Realizing that many non-Quakers wished to be involved on an equal basis in the Friends' humanitarian work, he created the Wider Quaker Fellowship to include them.

At its inception, the AFSC took up the cause of conscientious objectors, promoting alternate humanitarian service for Americans who objected to bearing arms during World War I. Following World War II, the AFSC and its British counterpart were presented with the Nobel Peace Prize. The citation read, "It is through silent assistance from the nameless to the nameless that [Quakers] have worked to promote the fraternity between nations. . . ."

Between the world wars, the AFSC responded to humanitarian crises in France, Russia, Poland, Serbia, Germany, and Austria. In the 1930s it assisted refugees to escape from Nazi Germany, provided relief for children in war-torn Spain, then fed refugees in occupied France while aiding victims of the London blitz. After World War II, the AFSC helped with humanitarian relief and reconstruction in Europe, India, China, and Japan. It mobilized to assist victims of the Korean War, the Hungarian Revolution, the Algerian War, and the Nigerian-Biafran War.

In the 1950s the AFSC created programs of social and technical assistance to developing nations, hoping to ease the tensions that lead to war. Concurrently, the AFSC acted to eliminate injustice in the United States, assisting Native Americans, Mexican Americans, migrant workers, and the poor.

Because its resources are more limited than those of the International Red Cross and other large relief agencies, the AFSC specializes in community building, remaining to rebuild communities long after the precipitating crises have passed.

In recent years, my wife has served as a consultant to the AFSC. Here is how Becky describes the way it assesses and responds to needs:

AN INSIDER'S APPRECIATION OF AFSC

"Visitors to the Cherry Street offices of the American Friends Service Committee in Philadelphia first encounter a statue of the Quaker martyr Mary Dyer. Executed by hanging on the Boston Commons in 1660 for her religious beliefs, Mary now sits primly on a bench, hands folded, eyes averted, looking serenely toward the future—a woman clearly at peace with the past. Hers is an appropriate image for the Religious Society of Friends, dubbed "Quakers" by a cynical seventeenth-century English magistrate. The name stuck, embraced by Friends. Since then Quaker numbers have radically declined to fewer than a half million worldwide. But the Friends' mission for justice and peace remains as strong as the day when Mary Dyer give her life for freedom of worship in the Puritan-dominated Massachusetts Bay Colony.

"Most people will tell you there is 'strength in numbers.' As a 'convinced Quaker'—one not born to the faith, but a Friend by choice—I disagree. I have the conceit to believe that one Quaker can be worth ten members of any other denomination when it comes to seeking justice and helping the disenfranchised. A bit of an exaggeration? Perhaps. But, as is so apparent in David's account, countless examples of individual Quaker effectiveness abound. It's the 'little faith that could.' Quakers require no crusades, no mass conversions, and no evangelists redeeming the unwashed to make our way in the world and beyond it. Besides, if Quakers are correct that there is 'that of God in everyone,' the unwashed are just fine with us, thank you very much.

"No single organization better represents George Fox's tenet of God's presence in everyone than the AFSC, which has earned the reputation of serving the unserved, regardless of race, creed, gender, or political persuasion. Its humanitarian aid arm, the Emergency and Materials Assistance Program (EMAP), provides assistance to victims of war and natural disasters both domestic and international, making no distinction among victims, and helping all who require aid. In recent years I had the honor of serving on its advisory committee, an experience I cherish.

"To emphasize how nondiscriminatory EMAP is, I once challenged the advisory committee with this question: 'If Saddam Hussein walked into one of our refugee centers asking for food and clothing, would we help him?' 'Yes,' came the answer. 'But is there that of God in him?' 'Yes' was the answer again. 'He just doesn't know it.'

"AFSC's relief efforts are hardly on the scale of the American Red Cross or the United Nations. Aware of its limitations, EMAP makes a thoroughgoing assessment of each situation before going in, ensuring that its limited number of personnel know where they can make the greatest impact. If it's sending school supplies to children in Baghdad or chess sets to Kosovar refugees (Kosovars are chess-mad), establishing safe havens for the Roma gypsy population during the Kosovo war, or penetrating the remote rural areas beyond New Orleans to aid Katarina victims, EMAP is there, always providing essentials such as food, clothing, and medical supplies but no sermons. Unlike other humanitarian agencies, it remains in the region long after others have folded their tents and departed.

"AFSC maintains strict neutrality in the midst of sectarian conflict, a beacon of compassion and no-nonsense practicality for all who suffer from hunger, persecution, and neglect, whether they be warriors or peacemakers. It may not trumpet its accomplishments on CNN, and you'll never see its chief administrator on the TV talk shows. In keeping with Quaker tradition, AFSC carries out its mission with quiet dignity.

"Perhaps it's true, at least in this instance: The best things *do* come in small packages."

QUAKERS IN THE PUBLIC INTEREST

In 1943, Quakers created the first ecumenical public interest lobby on Capitol Hill in the nation's capital. The Friends Committee on National Legislation (FCNL) is neither a political action committee nor a special interest lobby. Rather, it advocates legislation and policy that reflect Quaker testimonies of peace, equality, opportunity, and integrity. The FCNL's priorities are established every year by an informal poll of 227 Quaker meetings across America. As you might imagine, its permanent agenda seeks the peaceful prevention of deadly conflict, extension of civil rights to all Americans, protection of the environment, and redistribution of taxes to meet pressing human needs.

Quakers are also represented by offices at the United Nations, both in New York and in Geneva. The Friends World Committee for Consultation, which enjoyed consultative status with the United Nations starting in 1948, was promoted to general status in 2002 as a tribute to expanding Quaker involvement internationally. The heightened status allows Friends to testify before the UN Economic and Social Council and to suggest agenda priorities. Quaker staffers also deal directly with multilateral organizations, including the World Trade Organization, the International Labor Organization, the World Bank, and the International Monetary Fund.

A grassroots effort embraced by thousands of individual Quakers across America currently promotes the creation of a U.S. Department of Peace that would devise nonviolent solutions to domestic and international conflicts, counterbalancing the U.S. Department of Defense. As currently conceived, the new cabinet-level department would operate on just 2 percent of the budget currently required by the Pentagon. Many non-Quakers are joined in the effort, and a bill to create the new federal agency continues to gain cosponsors in Congress.

John Woolman, the Quakers' uncanonized saint, concluded his celebrated *Journal* with a sentiment that, despite its quaint eighteenth-century wording, expresses the faith, hope, and motivation of contemporary Quakers and their wish for all Americans:

> In this journey a labor hath attended my mind, that the ministers among us may be preserved in the meek, feeling life of truth, where we may have no desire but to follow Christ and to be with him, that when he is under suffering, we may suffer with him, and never desire to rise up in dominion, but as he, by virtue of his own spirit, may raise us.

"The ministers among us" to whom Woolman refers are not restricted to an exclusive elite but encompass all Friends and, by extension, all Americans. We are, each and every one of us, meant to minister to one another.

Perhaps that will be one outcome as the Quakers continue to reinvent America by perpetuating their age-old values, among them simplicity, integrity, responsibility, self-discipline, silence, a hatred of hypocrisy and pretension, and a stubborn adherence to honesty even in the face of persecution.

If Friends have one dogma to share with all Americans, it is this: that the truth will make us free.

Acknowledgments

$\mathcal{A}$s a journalist, I have long since reconciled myself to being a reporter rather than an innovator. I share life with a spouse who writes captivating novels, combining research with ingenious imagination. By contrast, I am limited to my own experience and to what I have learned from others.

I read Daniel J. Boorstin's *The Americans* decades ago, but it was only when I started to write about religious utopian movements in America that I was struck by what the historian had to say about the Quakers' pivotal role in the formation of the American character. Revisiting *The Americans* suggested the title of this book.

Coming to Quakerism late in life, I have had to absorb quickly just what I got myself into. Fortunately, my wife has been a Friendly companion as well as my best friend, sharing this adventure with me.

As an undergraduate at Knox College in Illinois, I was exposed to Quaker values by the late Elton Trueblood during compulsory chapel lectures. At the time, I found them charming but not compelling. Later, I devoured *Enthusiasm* by the late Catholic chaplain of Oxford University Ronald Knox and was moved by its admiring portrait of Quaker founder George Fox.

The Quakers are such a tidy group of people that I have already enjoyed the good fortune of meeting some whose books have most influenced me: the Quaker historian John Punshon, whose book *Portrait in Grey* is required reading. Also Robert Lawrence Smith, whose memoirs are titled *A Quaker Book of Wisdom*. He is the retired headmaster of Sidwell Friends School in the nation's capital.

J. Brent Bill (*Holy Silence*) has hosted me at Indiana's Earlham School of Religion, and Max L. Carter (*Minutiae of the Meeting*) offered a similar welcome at North Carolina's Guilford College, which he serves as Quaker chaplain. I continue to be indebted to them.

I have not had the pleasure of meeting Brandeis University historian David Hackett Fischer, whose massive study of early British migration to America, *Albion's Seed*, is definitive. My opening essay leans heavily on the nearly 200 pages he devoted to Quaker colonial life and values. It is more than fair to say that I would not have attempted this book had I not been introduced to Fischer's study by my wife.

Thanks to my editor, John Loudon, for getting these words into print and making them accessible to readers. And I am grateful to my fellow Friends of the Alexandria, Virginia, Monthly Meeting, in whose silence, simplicity, and hospitality I am privileged to participate.

I am especially grateful to my wife for her wisdom, encouragement, and truth telling, especially when my flights of fancy need to be brought down to earth. My profiles of Susan B. Anthony and Elizabeth Fry are based on Becky's lectures on prominent Quaker women, and she supplied an appreciation of the work of the American Friends Service Committee.

★ ★ ★

Because Quakers share the same spirit while decrying dogmas, I have paid scant attention to differences among contemporary Friends. Diversity does not mean divisiveness. But it may be useful for readers unfamiliar with Friends to grasp the richness of their diversity. Basically, Quaker congregations are classified as either programmed (and pastoral) or unprogrammed.

In this book, I have concentrated on unprogrammed worship—silence interrupted on occasion by a member moved by the Spirit. Unprogrammed Friends welcome seekers who do not necessarily consider themselves to be Christians.

Programmed worship, by contrast, has an order of worship similar to mainstream Protestant congregations. These Quakers strictly affirm the Christian faith and Church and make use of part time pastors, typically taken from the congregation. Their places of worship often resemble simple churches or chapels. These Friends refer to themselves as evangelical and still send missionaries to the Third World.

Perhaps a third of American Quakers and most Friends in the developed world are unprogrammed, whereas most congregations of Friends in the Third World are programmed.

Despite their diversity, they are Friends to one another and to all God's creation.

Bibliography

Barclay, Robert. *Collected Works*. Philadelphia: Benjamin Stanton, 1831.

Bill, J. Brent. *Mind the Light: Learning to See with Spiritual Eyes*. Brewster, Mass.: Paraclete Press, 2006.

———. *Holy Silence: The Gift of Quaker Spirituality*. Brewster, Mass.: Paraclete Press, 2005.

———. *Imagination and Spirit: A Contemporary Quaker Reader*. Richmond, Ind.: Friends United Press, 2002.

Boorstin, Daniel J. *The Americans: The Colonial Experience*. New York: Vintage, 1958.

Brinton, Howard H. *The Pendle Hill Idea*. Wallingford, Pa.: Pendle Hill, 1950.

Fischer, David Hackett. *Albion's Seed: Four British Folkways in America*. New York: Oxford University Press, 1989.

Foster, Richard J. *Celebration of Discipline: The Path to Spiritual Growth*. San Francisco: HarperSanFrancisco, 1998.

Foster, Richard J., and Emilie Griffin, eds. *Spiritual Classics*. San Francisco: HarperSanFrancisco, 2000.

Gulley, Philip. *For Everything a Season: Simple Musings on Living Well*. San Francisco: HarperSanFrancisco, 2001.

Hamm, Thomas D. *The Quakers in America*. New York: Columbia University Press, 2006.

———. *Earlham College: A History 1847–1997*. Bloomington: Indiana University Press, 1997.

Hartog, Jan de. *The Lamb's War*. New York: HarperCollins, 1980.

Herberg, Will. *Protestant, Catholic, Jew*. Garden City, N.Y.: Doubleday Anchor, 1960.

Jones, Rufus M. *Quakerism: A Spiritual Movement*. Philadelphia: Philadelphia Meeting of Friends, 1963.

Kelly, Thomas R. *A Testament of Devotion*. New York: Harper & Row, 1941.

Knox, Ronald, *Enthusiasm: A Chapter in the History of Religion.* Notre Dame, Ind.: University of Notre Dame Press, 1994.

Lewis, C. S. *A Grief Observed.* San Francisco: HarperSanFrancisco, 2001.

McCullough, David. *1776.* New York: Simon & Schuster, 2005.

Michener, James. *Chesapeake.* New York: Random House, 1978.

Newby, James R. *Elton Trueblood: Believer, Teacher, and Friend.* San Francisco: Harper & Row, 1990.

Pascal, Blaise. *Thoughts.* The Harvard Classics, vol. 48. New York: P. F. Collier & Son, 1909.

Punshon, John. *Reasons for Hope: The Faith and Future of the Friends Church.* Richmond, Ind.: Friends United Press, 2001.

———. *Portrait in Grey: A Short History of the Quakers.* London: Quaker Home Service, 1984.

Reisman, David. *The Lonely Crowd.* New Haven, Conn.: Yale University Press, 1950.

Smith, Robert Lawrence. *A Quaker Book of Wisdom.* London: Victor Gollancz, 1998.

Steere, Douglas V. *Friends and Worship.* Philadelphia: Friends General Conference, 1999.

Steere, Douglas V., and Jeannie Crawford-Lee. *Dimensions of Prayer.* Nashville: Upper Room Books, 1997.

Thoreau, Henry David. *Walden.* Philadelphia: Running Press, 1990.

Thurman, Howard. *Jesus and the Disinherited.* Boston: Beacon Press, 1996.

Trueblood, D. Elton. *The Incendiary Fellowship.* New York: HarperCollins, 1995.

West, Jessamyn. *The Friendly Persuasion.* New York: Harcourt, 1940.

Whitney, Janet. *John Woolman: American Quaker.* Boston: Little, Brown, 1942.

Woolman, John. *The Journal of John Woolman.* The Harvard Classics, vol. 1. New York: P. F. Collier & Son, 1909.

Yount, David. "Religion, the Eternal Growth Industry." *Washington Post*, 4 January 2004, pp. B1–B2.

———. *The Future of Christian Faith in America.* Minneapolis: Augsburg Books, 2004.

———. "Reflections of a Convinced Friend." *Friends Journal*, January 2003, pp. 22–24.

———. "Why Did the Quakers Stop Quaking?" *Quaker Life*, March 2002, pp. 12–13.

———. "Anticipating Eternity." *Potomac Review*, Winter 1999–2000, pp. 30–35.

———. *Ten Thoughts to Take into Eternity.* New York: Simon & Schuster, 1999.

———. *Spiritual Simplicity.* New York: Simon & Schuster, 1997.

Index

152 *Index*

2 Corinthians, 66; Galatians, 39;
Genesis, 27, 52–55; Isaiah, 41,
125; John, 27–28, 40, 53, 99;
Luke, 74, 96; Mark, 115;
Matthew, 39, 40, 47, 57, 61, 70,
98, 110; Romans, xxi, 66, 67, 87,
101; Sermon on the Mount, 47,
61, 108
Bill, J. Brent, 137, 146
Bill of Rights, 2, 14–15, 85
Black Beauty (Sewell), 128
Blake, William, 119
Blue-Collar Journal (Coleman), 136
Book of Common Prayer, 87
Boorstin, Daniel J., *2,* 80, 136–37,
145
born-again experience, 21, 38, 58, 102
Browning, Elizabeth Barrett, xviii
Browning, Robert, xiv, xviii, 22
Brown v. Board of Education, 130
Buford, Ron, 29–30
business ethic, 10
business meetings, 107

A Call to Be Vital (Jones), 42
capital punishment, 13, 16, 78, 108,
109, 133
Carter, Max L., 146
Catt, Carrie Chapman, 130
causes, devotion to, 120–21
Celebrations of Discipline (Foster), 140
Charles II, 78
Chesapeake (Michener), 138
Chesterton, G. K., 38, 41, 99, 116
children, 5–7, 74–76
Chopin, Frederic, xviii
Christian Peacemaker Team, ix
Church for the Fellowship, 129
civil rights, 129–30
Civil War, 132
clergy, Quaker view of, xxii, 44,
56–57, 84, 104, 107

clothing, 9, 106
Coffin, Levi, 128–29
Coleman, John R., 136
Coleridge, Samuel Taylor, xxiv
College of Philadelphia (University
of Pennsylvania), 83, 135
colonies: American Revolution, x, 83,
125–26; France and Spain, war
with, 81–82. *See also* Pennsylvania
Common Sense (Paine), x
community building, 141
conflict resolution, 12–13
congregational worship, 7
conscience, 6, 14, 71
conscientious objectors, 76, 108,
140–41
consolation, 95
Constitution, U.S., 2, 14–17, 85
construction, 4, 7
contemplatives, xiv
convincement, xxi–xxiv, 20–21; of
Fox, 21, 57–59, 61–63, 136;
repentance and, 57–60
Cooper, Gary, 105, 138
creeds, Quaker view of, xxi–xxii,
22–23, 51, 56–57, 69, 80,
100–101, 107, 135
crime and punishment, 13, 132–34
Croese, Gerald, 44
Crusades, 76

Dante, 31
darkness, symbol of, 31–33
Daughters of Temperance, 131
Dead Sea Old Testament, 48
death, 7, 87–88; fear of, 93–96; as
natural and inevitable, 89, 93–94;
near-death experiences, xviii–xix,
31, 89; obituaries, 91–93; of
parents, 89; technology confers
virtual immortality, 90–91. *See
also* afterlife; eternity

About the Author

David Yount writes the nationally syndicated column "Amazing Grace" and hosts a weekly cable television program. He regularly appears in the media and is the author of nine books, including *What Are We to Do? and Be Strong and Courageous*. He lives in Montclair, Virginia.

Visit the author on the Internet at www.erols.com/dyount.

He answers readers at P.O. Box 2758, Woodbridge, VA, 22195.

His most recent syndicated columns can be read at www.scrippsnews.com.

Dr. Yount maintains a limited speaking schedule on the subjects of his books and columns and leads retreats and quiet days.

If your local newspaper does not carry his Scripps Howard column, "Amazing Grace," ask your editor to consider it.